The Open Sore
of a CONTINENT

The Open Sore
of a CONTINENT

~~~~~~

A Personal Narrative of the Nigerian Crisis

Wole Soyinka

NEW YORK • OXFORD • OXFORD UNIVERSITY PRESS • 1996

Dedicated to the memory of
Dr. Tai Solarin, conscience of the nation,
who walked a last "step or two" with that nation
on June 30, 1994, and slept the day after

Oxford University Press

Oxford   New York
Athens   Auckland   Bangkok   Bogotá   Bombay
Buenos Aires   Calcutta   Cape Town   Dar es Salaam
Delhi   Florence   Hong Kong   Istanbul   Karachi
Kuala Lumpur   Madras   Madrid   Melbourne
Mexico City   Nairobi   Paris   Singapore
Taipei   Tokyo   Toronto

and associated companies in
Berlin   Ibadan

Published by Oxford University Press, Inc.,
198 Madison Avenue, New York, New York 10016

Oxford is a registered trademark of Oxford University Press

Library of Congress Cataloging-in-Publication Data

Soyinka, Wole.
The open sore of a continent : a personal narrative of the
Nigerian crisis / by Wole Soyinka.
p. cm.   ISBN 0-19-510557-5
1. Soyinka, Wole—Homes and haunts—Nigeria. 2. Soyinka, Wole—
Political and social views. 3. Authors, Nigerian—20th century—
Biography. 4. Nigeria—Politics and government—1960– I. Title.
PR9387.9.S6Z473 1996
882—dc20
[B]   96-8757

1 3 5 7 9 8 6 4 2

Printed in the United States of America
on acid-free paper

~~~~~~

Acknowledgments

*T*he contents of this volume, in the obligatory W. S. fashion, have been given in part, and the parts in variations and combinations around the main theme on different occasions both in Nigeria and abroad. They came together in a series of three public lectures as an attempted cohesive account of an event and its portents within the context of a continent, and of external histories, thanks to a residency stint in Harvard University with which, as it happens, I have a very understanding relationship. To Harvard President Neil Rudenstein, my former student, friend, and colleague Henry Louis (Skip) Gates Jr., and the staff of the DuBois Institute of Harvard—JoAnne Kendall and company—my sincere appreciation for that breathing space sorely needed after my "Rambo" departure from the Nigerian nation space.

I must not miss this opportunity to express also especially fervent appreciation to that ill-understood institution called UNESCO for its spontaneous moral and practical support of the beleaguered citizen of a member state that chose to act contrary to its international undertakings and membership code of conduct. I little realized when, as chairman of the UNESCO-affiliated International Theatre Institute, I had to preside over meetings involving problems of colleagues from some totalitarian states, that a few years thence I would also become the subject of such concerns. To Director-General Federico Mayor, Henri Lopez, his long-suffering secretary, Madame Josette Blot, and other staff of UNESCO, I wish to confess how unexpected and overwhelmed I have been by their solidarity and solicitude, and strategies for practical upliftment. Whichever ironic paths we find ourselves, individually, obliged to take to restore that benighted nation Nigeria to a humanistic course, and make her once again a worthy partner in the ideals for which UNESCO was founded I am unlikely to forget the reality of an extended family of global culture that one tends to take for granted.

There are many others, of course, more than deserving of mention, whose identities must remain, for now, undisclosed.

The irony of the date on which the above is written has just registered: It is *Independence* Day in another people's land, the United States of America.

London   W. S.
July 4, 1995

Contents

Introduction

*I*t would be difficult today to think of a more appropriate introduction to the contents of this volume than the following article, which was first published in the Nigerian media as far back as June 1994.

The Last Despot and the End of Nigerian History?

There was once a thriving habitation of some half a million people in southeastern Nigeria, the land of the Ogoni. It is an oil-producing area that has suffered much ecological damage. That damage has received world publicity largely due to the efforts of a feisty and passionate writer named Ken Saro-Wiwa, himself an Ogoni. A leader of the Movement for the Salvation of the Ogoni People, MOSOP, he exposed the plight of Ogoni to the United Nations Minorities Council, calling for the recognition of the Ogoni people as one of the world's endangered minorities. He agitated for compensation for damaged crops, polluted fishing ponds, and the general destruction of what was once an organic economic existence of his people.

That at least was in the beginning, some two or three years ago. Now, Ken Saro-Wiwa is held in chains in a hidden prison, incommunicado. He is seriously ill—he suffers from a heart condition—and is totally at the mercy of a gloating sadist, Major Paul Okutimo, a self-avowed killer and torturer of the military species, specially selected for the task of total "pacification" of Ogoniland. Saro-Wiwa's people have taken to the surrounding forests and mangrove swamps to survive. Those who remain in townships and villages are subjected to arbitrary displacement, expropriation of their property, violence on their persons, and the rape of their womanhood. Ogoniland has been declared a "military zone" under the direct rule of a "Task Force on Internal Security." Within this enclave, reporters, foreign or local, are made unwelcome and, in some cases, brutalized. In any case, the stable of an effective Nigerian press is being constantly reduced through illegal closures by the police on orders from the military. Before long, even those who penetrate the iron curtain of Sani Abacha's militarized enclave will have no media through which to remind the Nigerian populace of the atrocities daily inflicted on their Ogoni compatriots.

One ongoing actuality of repression very easily obscures another; it is a familiar and understandable pattern, one that dictatorships, especially of the most cynical kind, exploit most effectively. For the majority of Nigerians, Ogoni is only some localized problem, remote from the immediate, overall mission of rooting out the military from Nigerian politics, rescuing the nation's wealth from its incontinent hands, and terminating, once and for all, its routine murders of innocent citizens on the streets of Lagos and other visible centers of opposition. The massacres in Ogoni are hidden, ill-reported.* Those that obtain the just publicity of horror, mostly in government-controlled media, are those that are attributed to the Ogoni leadership movements, such as MOSOP.

Yet the accounts of such incidents and careful investigations lead to more than mere suspicions of dirty tricks, of covert military operations designed to discredit the leadership, throw the movement in disarray, and incite ethnic animosity between the Ogoni and their neighbors, thus instigating an unceasing round of bloodletting. The ambush of a passenger boat whose occupants were machine-gunned to death bore all the professional sophistication of a military operation, while the massacre, in broad daylight, of four prominent Ogoni leaders by supposed Ogoni militant youths has raised serious questions about the real identity of the instigators and indeed perpetrators of these crimes.

In any case, months after that last-mentioned atrocity, one that was laid at the door of rivals within that leadership, Ken Saro-Wiwa and others are still held in detention, under inhuman conditions, without a charge and without any indication of the slightest intention of bringing them to trial. It is impossible to believe that the forces of law and order do not know just who committed this open crime before hundreds of witnesses. It serves the purposes of Abacha's government, however, to portray Ogoni leadership as a bloodthirsty lot with no further mission than to

---

*Nearly a year after this was first published in Nigeria, the officer in question, Paul Okutimo, has rendered all further comment superfluous through his performance at a televised press conference. This was broadcast on channel 4, British Broadcasting Corporation (BBC), which has made recordings available.

settle their internal strife in the most public and brutal manner. It justifies the continued saturation of Ogoniland with military killer squads, exempt from any control or accountability.

Ogoniland is the first Nigerian experimentation with "ethnic cleansing," authorized and sustained by the Nigerian despot, General Sani Abacha! His on-the-spot operatives, Lieutenant Colonel Dauda Komo and Major Paul Okutimo, are Nigeria's contribution to the world's shameful directory of obedience to orders over and above the call of duty. The so-called Task Force on Internal Security is doomed to be Abacha's sole legacy to the nation, Nigeria's yet-unheralded membership card for the club of the practitioners of "ethnic cleansing."

Even if the following proves a further dent in Ogoni self-esteem, however, I am obliged to inform these victims that their agony is not an end in itself but a mere prelude, indeed a model exercise toward the far more thorough subjugation that is planned for other parts of Nigeria, also in the south, areas that do not even produce petroleum or indeed have any crucial industry that routinely feeds the rapacity of the Nigerian military class and its collaborators. Ogoniland is, alas, only the model space for the actualization of a long-dreamt totalitarian onslaught on the more liberated, more politically sophisticated sections of the Nigerian polity, which have dared expose and confront the power obsession of a minuscule but obdurate military-civilian hegemony. Ogoni people are, alas, only the guinea pigs for a morbid resolution of this smouldering inequity that was insti-tuted by the British as they planned for their departure. The beneficiaries remain, till today, a minority made up of a carefully nurtured feudal oligarchy and their pampered, indolent, and unproductive scions.

The carefully propagated myth of an uncritical political soli-darity within this section of the populace, the "north," was not just recently exploded, however. Its falsity was made manifest in earlier elections—1979 and 1983, especially. But these were so blatantly rigged by that same desperate minority and their mutual-interest partners of the south, that the positive (nationalist) signals were easily drowned in the hue and cry that followed. So, in a sense, it was not until the national elections of June 12, 1993, that the collapse of that fiction became irrefutable, thanks to the conduct of those elections, which was universally acclaimed a model of fairness, order, and restraint.

The pattern of voting also made it abundantly clear to the entire world that the so-called gulf between the north and the south was a deliberate invention of a minor, power-besotted leadership and its divisive gamesmanship. There is indeed a line of division in the north, but it is drawn between the workers, peasants, civil servants, petty traders, students, and the unemployed on the one hand and the parasitic elite and feudal scions on the other. These last, the beneficiaries of that ancient deception, are now traumatized. They cannot cope with this stark revelation of a nationalist political consciousness, so triumphantly manifested in the elections of June 12, 1993.

Their first reaction was astonishingly principled, and that should have served as an ominous warning. Their recognized leaders—including former presidential candidates—acknowledged defeat, gracelessly in some cases but courageously, even with a sense of relief in others. After the initial noises of realism and surrender to a popular, democratic will, the reprobates of the old order recovered their breath and recollected their endangered interests, regrouped, and ranged themselves behind a moldy concept of an eternal right to governance and control. The latest instrument of their feudal, despotic will is General Abacha, the last in the line of the reign of deception, of obfuscating rhetoric and cant in the service of a straightforward will to domination by an anachronistic bunch of social predators. Their notion of a historic mandate of power is not only warped and mindless; it may prove terminal to the existence of the nation if its most faithful facilitator to date, Abacha, succeeds in clinging to office for much longer. That is our reading of this crisis of nation being, and then Nigeria goes down as yet another forgotten smear in the geographical atlas of the world.

Of late, the Nigeria media have virtually waxed hysterical over the increasing arrogance and obduracy of this minority, thanks largely to the boastful performances of their most disreputable members. One notorious example is the lately returned fugitive Umaru Dikko, the task force specialist on rice importation, who barely escaped being crated back to Nigeria to face military justice under General Muhamadu Buhari. In denouncing the activities of this minority, described variously and often imprecisely as the Sokoto Caliphate, the Northern Elite, the Kaduna Mafia, the Hausa-Fulani oligarchy, the Sardauna Legacy, the Dan Fodio Jihadists, et cetera, what is largely lost in the passion and outrage is that they do constitute a minority—a dangerous, conspiratorial, and reactionary clique, but a minority just the same. Their tentacles reach deep, however, and their fanaticism is the secular face of religious fundamentalism.

But it is not just in the Nigerian free media that this minority's tyranny is discussed; and perhaps, before it is too late, our nettled general of the occupation forces of media houses will be made to realize this. Public debate—in such places as bars, bus stops, markets, garages, staff and student clubs, government offices (largely in the south, naturally)—has catapulted the activities of this minority to the heart of the national crisis, resulting in questioning the presumption (and June 12 affirmation) of the nation as a single entity. And the military, by its sectarian alliance with these claimants of divine attribution of power, has lost the last vestiges of any claims to neutrality in all areas of the contest for civic power. On June 23, 1993, the day of the arbitrary annulment of the national presidential election, the military committed the most treasonable act of larceny of all time: It violently robbed the Nigerian people of their nationhood! *A profound trust was betrayed, and only a community of fools will entrust its most sacred possession—nationhood—yet again to a class that has proven so fickle, so treacherous and dishonorable.*

Therefore, those who still advocate that Sani Abacha has inaugurated his own program of transition to civil rule from a "sincere interest of the (Nigerian) nation at heart" are bewildering victims of a carefully nurtured propaganda that began with the erstwhile dictator of Nigeria, General Ibrahim Badamasi Babangida. It was this propaganda, waged on an international scale and funded to the tune of millions of dollars, that enabled quite a few, normally intelligent analysts at the Africa desk of foreign powers to propose that the expensive, impossibly tortuous transition-to-democracy program of Abacha's predecessor was a well-considered, disinterested program that objectively recognized the peculiar nature of Nigerian politicians, to which abnormality the good general was merely responding.

These foreign powers thus became disposed to blame all the various setbacks of the transition program—in reality custom-built for failure—on the irredeemable nature of the politicians themselves. And it was only to counter this political incorrigibility that the peculiar genius of Babangida was sublimely suited—all in the interest, naturally, of the nation itself. Now Abacha adds insult to injury by inaugurating his own never-never transition program, posturing over an imagined nation of placid mules at whom he tosses threats and orders from the heights of Aso Rock, our Abuja version of Mount Olympus. Nigerians are not inclined to embark once again on the labors of Sisyphus.

But I. B. B. was at least original. What Nigeria is confronting today is a species of mimic succession that considers itself innovative. The imposition of a Constitutional Conference in 1994 by General Sani Abacha as a "solution" to the artificial crisis developed from a free and fair election is really a pitiable compliment to I. B. Babangida, who at least played that con game with panache, milking it eventually to death. In Abacha's hands, it is a squeezed-dry, humorless patent for any would-be dictator. It is a fair assessment of the IQ of Abacha that he actually imagines that this transparent ploy for self-perpetuation would fool the market woman, the roadside mechanic, the student, factory worker, or religious leader of whatever persuasion. Even the village idiot must marvel at such banal attempts to rival a disgraced predecessor.

Nigerians simply do not believe for one single moment in this conference, not even the propagandists who must churn out the government line, and even less the volunteers and conscripts he has gathered together in Abuja for this non-event. The participants are mostly economically exhausted politicians who cannot resist a six-month sabbatical without obligations, all expenses paid and then some; they are chronic wheelers and dealers looking for a quick financial handout from the inexhaustible (but drastically devalued) government purse, politicians seeking a free and painless venue for some horse trading in preparation for the resumption of civilian party politics. There are of course also the antidemocratic diehards, the aforesaid guardians of the very private precinct of power, for whom the very notion of an actualized June 12 election, that declaration of national unity, must be expunged from memory for all eternity. And we must not forget those who have joined the ride in the practical (and sometimes idealistic) belief that "if you cannot join them, beat them at their own game." These last have lately discovered that the majority of the delegates cannot be beaten because their rules of engagement are nonexistent and their purposes run on parallel rails. Several have since quit.

Not to be forgotten—however academic it may sound, given the nature of military rule—is the fact that Abacha's administration is patently illegal and has been thus proclaimed by the Nigerian law courts. What is of special interest in that court decision, however, is that the judgment was based on the military's own legislation. Abacha's "legitimacy," in his own pronouncement, derived from the rules of succession that governed the soap opera "interim government" of Ernest Sonekan. That interim government was declared illegal by the courts—again based on the provisions of the military government's own legislation. Abacha's so-called succession was therefore a claim in legal and constitutional void.

We have gone to court once again to obtain a separate declaration on Abacha himself. This move involves more than an academic exercise, however. The Nigerian populace is being primed for a campaign of comprehensive civil disobedience. They are being reinforced in their conviction that their cause and their acts are backed by law; that it is an outlaw who presently inhabits Aso Rock; that his closures of media houses and confiscation of passports are illegal—nothing but plain thuggery; that his seizure and operation of the nation's treasury and revenues are nothing but acts of banditry; that his imagined authority to try anyone for treason is the ultimate ridicule of a judiciary that his very presence in Abuja and contemptuous flouting of court orders subvert; that his detention of any Nigerian citizen is nothing but the hostage-taking tactics of two-a-penny terrorists . . . that, in short, he may exercise power through the gun, but he lacks authority even in the most elastic sense of the word, and that this emptiness must be made increasingly manifest in public acts of rejection.

The self-styled Constitutional Conference is therefore nothing but another expensive charade that all subscribers, Abacha most of all, recognize as being instituted to serve every purpose but that for which it has been named. It is itself illegal. We called successfully for a boycott of its elections, and it was a mere

350,000 souls that came out to save it from a total farce. We need only compare this to the 14 million voters that voted in Bashorun Moshood Abiola as Nigeria's president. And of the membership of this Abacha assembly, close to a full third were his (and his cabal's) personal nominees. Nigerians, not surprisingly, treat the entire proceedings as yet another circus of political mutants and opportunists, promoted by a frantic bunch of aliens who only happen to hold Nigerian passports.

Abacha's March 1994 address to the nation, one that reemphasized his determination to decide our destiny through this stillborn conference, was of course not unexpected. This particular despot differs from his predecessor in his inability to cope with more than one line of thought or anticipate more than one course of action or response in any given month. His address, however, fell short, for now, of the scorched-earth policy that we had expected him to declare—the proscription of the striking trade unions, imposition of a state of emergency, the closure of more media houses, and, yes, even detention camps for dissidents.

The blueprint for these measures has been worked out, and military units—veterans of random slaughter of civilians—even deployed to opposition strongholds for a ruthless clampdown on the populace. The necessary decree was drafted—no, not from the attorney general's office (that misguided lawman has long been sidelined)—but from the presidency itself, where the secretary to the government, one Alhaji Aminu Saleh, an unabashed "capo" of the notorious minority, has taken over the functions of law drafting, recruiting private lawyers to do the dirty work that the AG had shown increasing reluctance to undertake. The government prosecutors of the president-elect, Bashorun M.K.O. Abiola were, for instance, lawyers recruited from private practice, contracted not by the attorney general's office but by Aminu Saleh. His bold, unchallengeable incursions into the zone of authority even of generals within the cabinet are already public knowledge.

It is necessary to alert the world now that this plan has merely been shelved, not abandoned. Abacha, let no one be in any doubt, has resolved to subjugate the strongholds of opposition in an even more ruthless manner than he did last year when, as Babangida's hatchet man, he succeeded in murdering over two hundred prodemocracy demonstrators. I was in the midst of these protesters on the second day, June 27. I witnessed the insensate shooting by Abacha's soldiers and mobile police and counted bodies in the Agege-Ipaja sector. But that was a bloody response to a specific situation. This time round, a far more systematic response has been outlined: Nigeria, especially the west and the oil-producing southeast, is to be "Ogonised" in a thoroughgoing blitz. The trade union leaders, the intellectual and professional opposition, are to be sequestered and subjected to absolute military control under the clones of the Dauda Komos and Paul Okutimos.

Abacha is resolved to spread the "Ogoni" solution throughout southern Nigeria. A minuscule being and matching mind, but with a gargantuan ego, he feels personally insulted by the resistance to his delusions and has sworn, if it came to the crunch, to "wipe out the very oil wells those labor unions are using to blackmail us." That statement is a very reliable quote. Abacha is out to out-Saddam Saddam Hussein's parting gift to Kuwait. Anyone who believes that Abacha will not kill the goose that lays the golden egg forgets that, in any case, the general's private barn is already bursting with a vast deposit from Nigeria's obliging goose.

Those who wish to understand the catastrophe toward which the Nigerian nation is being propelled will do well to study the personalities of the present and the immediate past Nigerian military despots. Babangida enjoyed power, enjoyed playing at and for power. The very politics of power was, for him, an intellectual challenge. Even the diabolism inherent in the phenomenon of power was something that he relished. Thus, bribery, manipulation, divisive tactics, cajolery, patronage, double-talk, the gloved fist, the attentive "listening" posture, consultation syndrome, the studying, nurturing, and exploitation of weaknesses, blackmail, back stabbing, the cultivation of seeming detachedness—that is, the ability to "referee" yet remain a contestant for political stakes, and so on—all these formed the armory of a wily politician nicknamed Maradona, whose fatal error was that he soon began to play against himself and scored his own goal.

Babangida's love of power was visualized in actual terms: power over Nigeria, over the nation's impressive size, its potential, over the nation's powerful status (despite serious image blemishes) within the community of nations. The potency of Nigeria, in short, was an augmentation of his own sense of personal power. It corrupted him thoroughly, and all the more disastrously because he had come to identify that Nigeria and her resources with his own person and personal wealth.

Not so Abacha. Abacha is prepared to reduce Nigeria to rubble as long as he survives to preside over a name—and Abacha is a survivor. He has proved that repeatedly, even in his internal contests with Babangida. Totally lacking in vision, in perspectives, he is a mole trapped in a warren of tunnels. At every potential exit he is blinded by the headlights of an oncoming vehicle and freezes. When the light has veered off, he charges to destroy every animate or inanimate object within the path of the vanished beam. Abacha is incapable of the faculty of defining that intrusive light, not even to consider if the light path could actually lead him out of the mindless maze.

Abacha has no *idea* of Nigeria. Beyond the reality of a fiefdom that has dutifully nursed his insatiable greed and transformed him into a creature of enormous wealth, and now of power, Abacha has no *notion* of Nigeria. He is thus incapable of grasping what is being said to him by some entity that speaks with the resolute voice of the Civil Liberties Organization, the Campaign for Democracy, the National Democratic Coalition, the market women, civil servants, student unions, labor unions, the press, and so forth. None of these could possibly be part of his Nigerian nation, and it is only by eliminating them *in toto*, by silencing such alien voices, that Nigeria can become the entity that he recognizes.

When Abacha took over from the interim government in November 1993, I warned that he would prove more ruthless than any dictator we have endured in the nation till now. At the beginning, it appeared that I was being proved an alarmist. Now, of course, we are seeing what matter he is made of, and the worst, I regret to say, is yet to come. Abacha will be satisfied only with the devastation of every aspect of Nigeria that he cannot mentally grasp, and that is virtually all of Nigeria. He will find peace and fulfillment only when the voices whose nation language he cannot interpret are finally silenced, only when, like the Hutus, he cuts off the legs of the Tutsis so that Nigeria is reduced to a height onto which he can clamber.

These voices, however, and the history that brought them into being, and with such resolve, have already ensured that Abacha is the last despot who will impose himself on the Nigerian nation. Of course, there will be others who will yield to temptation and attempt to tread the same path of illusion, but their careers will be so short-lived that they will hardly be noticed in passing. The strategy of the present struggle is such that the people are attaining an unprecedented level of self-worth within a national being that defines anti-democrats as treasonable conspirators— and precludes any future automatic submission to the sheerest suspicion of military despotism, even of a messianic hue.

The danger, the very real danger, however, is in the *character* of this last torchbearer for military demonology, the puny Samson whose arms are wrapped around the pillars, ready to pull down the edifice in his descent into hell. That hell that is Ogoniland today is the perception of nation compatibility of which Abacha's mind is capable. What does not readily yield to his obsessive self-aggrandizement both in power and possessions is alien and must be subjugated and "sanitized." In Sani Abacha's self-manifesting destiny as the last Nigerian despot, we may be witnessing, alas, the end of Nigerian history.

A Flawed Origin—But No Worse than Others

I am obliged to concede that the overall tenor of my remarks could be easily construed as a requiem for what we know as the nation of Nigeria, so let me caution at the beginning that this is not my intention. The chain of political crises in Nigeria is, however, tied, recognizably, to the goal of evolving into a nation, and it is therefore unavoidable that we examine, in the light of such perennial crises, just how valid are the definitions of nationhood in the first place, and whose definitions these are, both in the conception and in the physical manifestation of the concept itself. This prompts a re-examination, at the very least, of the process of nationhood itself and its fortunes in contemporary experience.

Having conceded that much, however, thanks to some responses from an earlier version of this lecture, I must also state at the outset that in Nigeria we may actually be witnessing a nation on the verge of extinction. There is no paradox whatever in all of this, if we would only picture a scenario between a doctor and a patient whose affliction may prove terminal. The physician is not thereby relieved of his Hippocratic oath but must confront the patient with his diagnosis and advise him on certain preventive measures. He might go even further and show the patient a chart of the internal systems of similar patients, worse off or not so advanced in physical decay, et cetera. The doctor, if he is extra conscientious, might advise the immediate family on how to help the patient survive, keeping tempting but harmful foods away from him (avoid the soda pop, the popcorn, the junk food, the greasy hamburger, or nouvelle cuisine), ensuring that he takes at least one bottle of wine a day, or whatever. As you can see, I am not really qualified as an authority in that department.

For many of us, this summarizes the motivations that induce one to continue to speak of a terminal case whose general consumption habits, to name just one aspect, have overqualified it for the cemetery of nations for the past two decades—that is, since after the Biafran civil war. When, for instance, we call upon the outside world to isolate a parasitic régime whose ravages merely expose the body's condition of the walking dead, to impose comprehensive sanctions against such a chronic afflic-tion, it is only because our medical analysts have concluded that further feeding along its customary diet critically endangers the already slim chances of recovery for the national body. Certain forms of fever need to be starved. Unfortunately, this concern appears to be misinterpreted by such régimes: They accuse us of attempting to starve the nation to death. In our very simple-minded worldview, we insist on the distinction between the people and the state.

But I am jumping the gun somewhat. We shall come later to what we believe the international community can do to save the

nation, not so much from itself as from the internal expropria-
tors of the national weal. We must advance to the complementary questions: Save it for what? Or, as what? As a nation? As
nations? As a satellite or satellites of other nation arrangements?
There are precedents, after all, in becoming a ward of the United
Nations, in some form or the other. That, certainly, is far less
extreme than some other prescriptions that one occasionally
encounters, both seriously and half-jokingly, within and outside
the nation in recent times—one such prescription being that only
a phase of recolonization will save the nation!

Whatever outlandish or original solutions do suggest themselves, we are thrown back on one question. It has become lately
insistent, and not merely for our continent but in the global
search for stability within what passes for national boundaries,
and, indeed, for ensuring civilized relationships and security
in daily transactions between neighbors. That question is: *When
is a nation?* The question could be phrased in several other
ways: For instance, what price a nation? Half a million lives
lost in brutish termination, within the cheap span of a mere
month, and for no discernable purpose but vengeance, a vengeance that is also opportunistic, since it harbors the unde-
clared goal of creating a Rwandan "nation" of pure Hutu breed?
What mores define a nation? Or indeed, what yardsticks? What
does the claim "I belong to this nation" mean to the individual,
and when did it begin to mean anything? For instance, to the
Ewe split between Ghana and Togo? Or the Albanians within
the former Yugoslavian borders? These are unavoidable details
of the terms in which I have posed the question, a version that is
meant to be summative. When, and this is what is demanded,
when are all the conditions present that make a nation? Can
they be upheld by objective tests? Or is a nation simply a
condition of the collective mind? Or will? A coerced state,
the objective manifestation of an individual will? A passive,

unquestioned habit of cohabitation? Or a rigorous conclusion that derives from history?

We must not even shy away from the possibility that a nation is a mere sentimental concept, unfounded in any practical advantages for its occupants. Or that the only hard fact that confers the status of nationhood on any human collectivity is its right to issue passports. We could simplify the issue and restrict ourselves to contemporary times, employing the club membership of the United Nations; when that organization chooses to admit you into its fold, does that unequivocally confer on you the status of nationhood? But what then of apartheid South Africa; did it cease to be a nation when it was expelled from the United Nations? The Boers would have a word or two to contribute in that context, guaranteed to be irreconcilable with the position of the oppressed black majority. Nationhood then may prove itself to be more complicated than the actualized sovereignty of any human grouping, not necessarily homogenous, for when, as in that last example, a distinctive minority exercises state power, controls national assets including choice lands that exclude but are contested by the majority, we find that we cannot totally evade the subjective actuality of nation being. An apt description of such actualities would be that of two human torsos in uneasy cohabitation within the same shirt. Even when such a phenomenon appears to be an "act of nature," as in Siamese twins, we know that the corrective ingenuity of the surgeon is often summoned as the arbiter of such a "natural" abnormality. What then shall we say of seeming abnormalities that are the product of human disingenousness, of adventurism? That they are immutable once fashioned into nation being or addressed as such?

We concede of course that solutions need not take such drastic forms as surgery, as is being currently proved by the miracle of that same South Africa. If the Boers had adopted a different strategy of separatism, committed to ridding themselves of the "problem" once and for all rather than the creation of landlocked Bantustan labor reservations, we could very easily be compelled today to live with several nations from that same South Africa. So when *is* a nation?

Even geographical coherence, within any arbitrarily elected measure of contemporaneity, does not appear to offer any certitudes. First there was India, and it included present-day Pakistan, uncomfortably sliced in half by what remained of India after Pakistan went its independent way. Before splitting up in turn into present-day Pakistan and Bangladesh, Pakistan, despite being thrust apart by the landmass of India, appeared to consider herself and be accepted by others as one nation—East and West Pakistan. For that duration at least, the factor of geographical separation did not noticeably vitiate the claims of a single national entity. Fortunately we need not journey from the African continent to find our examples: Various unions have attempted to redefine their nation being on that landmass—the Ghana-Guinea-Mali Union, the even shorter-lived United Arab Republic of Libya and Egypt, or the more recently abrogated semi-union between Senegal and Gambia.

Nation making from the top (what I earlier referred to as the objective manifestation of the will of one individual or a handful of individuals) never does, however, appear to have much staying power: witness the sanguinary face-off between North and South Yemen in recent times. Plebiscites—genuine plebiscites, that is—appear to stand a better chance. We had an instructive experience of it in our history when a slice of eastern Nigeria decided to go with Cameroon. That section is still very much part of the Cameroon, whatever second thoughts the population might have had, periodically, about that decision. Today, however, I suspect that one serious look at the condition of the Nigerian nation would persuade them that they were indeed wise and fortunate to have sought their fortune elsewhere.

We shall leave out for now the problem of Bakassi, the oil-rich peninsula to the southeast of Nigeria that many outside the African continent may not have heard of, but one that has resulted in a military standoff between Nigeria and the Cameroon, with the French conducting naval maneuvers in that region—purely by accident, of course—in 1993. The peninsula was apparently signed off to the Cameroon by General Yakubu Gowon as a bribe or reward for President Ahmadou Ahidjo's support of the federal cause during the Biafran war. Now, Nigeria claims that this transfer was never ratified by the military council and is therefore of no legal effect. Cameroon, backed naturally by France, insists that the agreement was not only binding but that it merely righted a previous wrong, since Bakassi had always been part of the Cameroon nation anyway. Neither side has ever stopped to savor the supreme irony of behaving in identical fashion to the European imperialist powers who parceled out the African nations among themselves, separating ancient communities and yoking others together without so much as a look at the humanity that actually peopled and cultivated the contested land!

The lesson we are obliged to extract from the contrast outlined between nation stitching from the top and its evolution from the base—that is, the latter as an expression of the will or habit and usage of peoples, even if imperfectly educed—is that the latter might provide us one of the clues to our central question, When is a nation? Could one of the conditions in resolving this sometimes emotive issue be the articulated or demonstrable decision by the polity that actually makes up the nation? I propose that we keep this possibility in mind as we go forward, which imposes on us a readiness to consider that invocation of the absence of such a stamp of accord throws any nation claim back into question, if only on the theoretical level. Whether we prefer to wait for the lurking Rwandas on the continent to materialize in the absence of such an accord is another matter altogether; until the explosion, we are at liberty to continue to take the European imperial will as the final arbiter in such matters of death and destruction. If we choose to confront reality, however, then I do suggest that many nations on the African continent are only in a state of limbo, that they exist in a halfway space of purgatory until, by mundane processes or through dramatic events, their citizens are enabled to raise the nation reality to a higher level, then even higher still, until it attains a status of irreversibility—either as paradise or hell.

There are of course many ways of arriving at a just answer to our basic question; indeed, a nation accord is not one that necessarily comes about by any formal or structured process, such as a plebiscite. A political entity that, for an appreciable period, has saluted a common flag, adopted a common anthem, a motto, or a common pledge for ceremonial or instructional occasions, a polity that uniformly loses its collective sense of proportion when its football team goes to battle, fights a war or two as one entity, flaunts a common passport, and pools and distributes its economic resources by some form of consensus, even where such a system of distribution is periodically challenged—I repeat, one that has, for an appreciable length of time, managed its affairs within the context of these unifying virtues or irrationalities—such an entity may indeed be deemed a nation by obvious status quo. Its categorization as such is contested neither from within nor without, and this of course is true of most nations that we refer to as such today. No one questions the nation status of France, Sweden, Japan, Ghana, Zambia, or Portugal. When we take the question to Portugal's Iberian neighbor, Spain, we are held up by the violent veto of the Basque separatist movement, which continues to insist that the nation that we are conditioned to regard as one Spain is, for them, two nations—the Basque and the rest! Six decades of repression and/

or blandishments in the name of unity have done nothing to mellow the Basque nationalist quest. Even Catalonia, whose language and culture were viciously repressed under General Francisco Franco, has only grudgingly, in recent times, accepted a less extreme relationship to mother Spain. Its language has, however, been resurrected, its literature flourishes in the once forbidden Catalan, just as any occasion is used to stress its distinct culture and nation origin.

As we seek to widen our examples, we find even more aggravating complications. Morocco, for instance: Is Morocco a nation? A decade or two ago, such a question would have sounded preposterous but since that nation made a grab for former Spanish Sahara, we now have to question where precisely lies the nation of Morocco. Clearly it cannot be that geographical space that includes the Saharouis region, contested by Polisario. And Turkey? The Kurds, with increasing militancy, question the nation space of that country. Indeed, the Kurds have inserted fissures in the nation claims not only of Turkey but of Iraq and Iran, just like the Armenians in the new nation-states of the former Soviet Union. This matter is far more serious, far more profoundly relevant to our quest. Not only do the Kurds battle for autonomous or semi-autonomous existence within these countries, they have gone back in their own history and re-proclaimed themselves a nation. They demand that the world redress the historically acknowledged pogrom of their people and the erasure of their nation actuality from the map of the world. The Kurds perceive themselves already as a nation, even as the Palestinians have done for decades as they move closer to the actualization of a nation dream too long deferred.

We are entering, it must be apparent by now, the possibility— not of a discovery—but of the recovery of a certain historical truth: that nation status has never been an absolute or a constant, that it has ever followed the politics of conflict, interest, alliances, power, and even accident. We know how the Middle East oil states came to be, a fact that was not missed by Saddam Hussein when he embarked on his misadventure and claimed Kuwait as an integral province of Iraq. The Yemens, Saudi Arabia, Qatar, Jordan, et cetera: Are these truly nations? Or, put the question another way: Could it also be claimed that they were always nations, albeit by another name, defined by another concept that was first ridiculed, then rehabilitated—with some emendations, of course, under European imperialism? If you reexamine the various properties that we have listed as being germane to the definition of a state (and I use that word loosely) we may find that the so-called tribal kingdoms or clan principalities that were later supplanted by European imperialist arrangements do indeed qualify for nation status. Even to the extent of securing recognition for their passports, or letters of authority that amounted to passports, for what is a passport anyway but a request that ease of passage and protection be offered to the bearer, at the behest of some authority under whose suzerainty the bearer of that document belongs?

The erstwhile Union of Soviet Socialist Republics, under its Communist structure, played a most fascinating game with its nationalities. Within the United Nations, these various entities— Georgia, Russia, Uzbekistan, Siberia, and so forth—existed and were recognized as individual nations, an arrangement that awarded the Soviet Union a few more votes than, shall we say, the United States of America, which presented a single national front despite her fifty states. Within the Soviet Union, however, we do know that during the monolithic reigns of Lenin and Stalin "the natives were restless." Ruthless as was the repression of nationalist claims, concessions had to be made from time to time to such stirrings, especially in the matter of culture and language. The "nationalities" question was one that never disappeared from Marxist literature; it certainly featured prominently, with much vituperation, in Lenin's and Engels's writings. Joseph Stalin's variations on the same theme were mostly written in blood, often on a genocidal scale.

Any unprogrammed visitor to the Soviet Union did not need to be told that there were various distinct nations within that iron-bound collective; even between Moscow and Leningrad, the difference, as they say, was clear. And when you found yourself in the more distinctly Asian states, strolled through the market of Samarkand, it did not require your tragi-romantic recollection of James Elroy Flecker's verse play *Hassan* to make you aware that you had plunged into a different culture and a different people, even a different time, from what you left behind in Moscow. This was not just a question of the natural differences between the culture of a capital city or a seat of central government and the rural regions—no, the very landscape, despite its disfigurement by the predictable structures of centralized party architecture, despite the uniform railway stations, the composite town halls and *palais des sports,* the joyless arenas conceded to art and folk cultures, and the "correct" postures and bloodless contacts that officialdom inflicted on you, despite these and a hundred tricks of programmed uniformity, the authentic face of Samarkand overrode these skin-deep afflictions and you experienced a national reality that was different from that of Kiev, Tbilisi, or even beautiful Leningrad. Do we then suggest that nation being is a matter of "soul," that a nation acquires its certificate of being when we experience a palpable uniqueness, an essence that is not subject to itemization? I doubt that that mystical dimension will satisfy anyone, yet it is not a negligible factor, unquantifiable, in attempting to differentiate one's response to the distinct national signatures of, shall we say, Ireland and England.

The choice of those two examples is of course deliberate. The bloody contest for the redefinition of the nation of Ireland remained unrelenting until the ceasefire in mid-1994, spilling over into the United Kingdom itself, as some of my affluent fellow Nigerians discovered, whenever an unfortunate coincidence of timing brought them out to their second homes, those exclusive shopping centers in London, during the Irish Republican Army (IRA) bombing campaign. That was one of those periods when they were prepared to swear that even Babangida's Nigeria was infinitely preferable to the haven they had sought abroad. The case of Northern Ireland has been singularly complicated, as the main Republic of Ireland itself, during the struggle, periodically expressed doubts about whether or not it actually wanted to absorb this violent space, in the event that the Protestant population eventually succumbed to guarantees that would make the unification demands of the IRA acceptable. It was—still is—an unusual situation: a national longing that has nowhere to go! It is somewhat more straightforward when a people simply demand their own independent being, not seeking to merge an identity with another but to imbue such an identity with its own sovereign status. Whatever the peculiarities of each of these and dozens of other lesser-known scenarios, we come up eventually against one chastening caveat: Is it really ever possible, in the secure dominion of our intellectual distances, to prescribe for any one of these expressions of the will to nationhood?

One of our former ministers of foreign affairs appeared to have attempted to do just that very stridently and confidently in his statements on Yugoslavia about three years ago. It was an exercise that I found truly astonishing. How could such an attitude be defended, I demanded in turn? Under what theory of development or philosophy of social evolution? Under what inviolable, universally applicable laws of excision, cohesion, and association? I couldn't help wondering at the time if he would not have begun to sing a different tune if he had been subjected to the very anguish that average Bosnians or Croatians were experiencing at that moment, the Moslems especially, trapped between the aggressive ambitions and program of "ethnic cleansing" of Greater Serbia and the equally nationalist determination of Croatia. What wouldn't he give then for a little parcel of land to call his own, independent of both! The truth is, any claim to absolutes in these matters is simply empty; conclusions are constantly contradicted by the very real, non-abstract humanity that inhabit these spaces. Every space that encloses humanity in sovereign claims is unique in at least a dozen aspects and thus no single law, no single body of criteria can answer "Valid" or "Invalid" to any claims for an independent nation being. Is it Eritrea that we shall presume has committed a crime against universal law? Or southern Sudan that is doomed to eternal damnation in the afterlife of nations for its three-decades-old war of separatist determination?

It is quite tempting, I admit, for a nation like mine to pose, as it sometimes does, as the Great Exemplar. Nothing fails like failure and nothing succeeds like success. We did fight a so-called war of unity and ended up intact—geographically at least. From that position it is easy to transfer the example of that implemented will to unity onto others, dismiss the unique circumstances of other contestants and patronize their anguish. The Nigerian geographical entity was indeed upheld, but was the *nation*? Is present-day Sudan a nation at all? That really ought to be the question, or at least that is one approach toward a comprehensive understanding of the Sudanese civil war. The tenacity with which a war is sustained, its duration, a readiness of the populace for endless sacrifice are not—let me hasten to add, *should* not be—the yardstick by which the credentials of nation readiness is judged, but it must certainly count toward our assessment. Other factors weigh just as heavily, but no one can deny that courage, resolve, suffering, and heroism do touch a chord in our humanity. If these properties, abundantly displayed by the southern

Sudanese, do not tilt the scale in the consideration of other factors—religious, racial, and economic—then our humanity is dead, and we are slaves of airy abstractions, of vaporous notions that are not grounded in the earth we tread, in its products, in the only species known to cultivate, exploit, and augment the resources of that earth. Between the creator hand and the created object of that hand, between the nurturing mind and the thought to which the mind gives birth, there can be no question of which one has primary existence and therefore primary claims. To encapsulate this in a familiar expression that, in this instance, has a singular poignancy for us, who owe our contemporary corporate existences to the intervention of the European world, "The oyinbo wey make pencil, na 'im also make erazer." If the hemorrhage within the nation boundary known as Sudan violates our commitment to humanity, then we must begin to think laterally from received orthodoxies.

The inviolability principle of national boundaries is therefore a fictitious concept, born out of nothing more substantial than faith, and therefore every bit as questionable for those of the rational world. And even those whose existence is bound by faith, especially of the religious kind, are cautious to deny specific boundaries to the provinces of heaven, hell, or purgatory. These are left severely to the imagination, free to be adjusted according to population proportions in the hereafter. When Satan launched his takeover bid against the forces of God, it was, after all, an attempt to unify the celestial provinces, if Milton's account in *Paradise Lost* is to be believed. This, however, proved one instance when the unity principle did not prove popular; the cultures, mores, and ethics of heaven and hell were simply incompatible, and a war of separate identities was won by the supposedly good side, while evil, on the side of unity, lost out ignominiously. Clearly the notion of unification for its own sake and at any price has been faulted even in the metaphysical realms, so where, then, in this entire universe are we to find the philosophy of wholes and parts that endows one, rather than the other, with immutable authority? The answer is Nowhere. Nowhere at all. It is we, the occupants of the whole or the part who must decide whether it serves our collective interest to stay together or pull apart. And we can only commence by a recourse to history, the quality of life in the present and the tangible advantages, as well as the projection that we can make into the future, stemming from today's realities in all fields of our human activity.

When I listen therefore to some pontificating voice declaring that the unity of Nigeria is non-negotiable, I detect only wooly or opportunistic thinking. What the speaker is saying is this: It suits me and mine to keep Nigeria a single entity. In a moment, we shall come to a remarkable instance of this unity fervor at its most banal, venal, and cynical. There is absolutely no foundation in the absolute for such a declaration. But it does serve, in a perverse way, to acknowledge the fact that when there is evident plurality of otherwise divergent, even irreconciliable interests actually baying the same chorus, we begin to sense the potential of such a polity as a nation in the making. I stress the role of divergences in the motivations of such nation clamor, for it enables us to address the obvious proposition: that a polity can actually become a nation simply by a guarantee or mechanism for the reconciliation of multiple interests within its historic or artificial bounds. Here is a frivolous instance.

At the initial stages of the doomed existence of the 1993 interim government—this was the puppet government set up as a cushion for the fall of Babangida, a ludicrous concoction that was rejected by nearly the entire nation—I was involved in an initiative to terminate that affliction as painlessly as could be managed. It entailed a number of meetings, and one took place in Lagos with a highly placed military official within the government. We analyzed the various options and the risks inherent both in those options as well as in the continuing existence of the Sonekan interim government charade. Naturally, we did not shy away from the probability of a civil war and the possible disintegration of the country as its consequence. It was as we examined that very real danger that I said to him, Look, I wear out passports at such an abnormal rate that I do not even wish to consider the prospect of having to devote more pages to visas just because I need to travel to Onitsha in the east or Maiduguri in the north.

My purpose was of course to bring some light relief to an intense discussion but, as with most jokes, this had a serious element to it. With all the imponderables that confronted the nation at the time, with all the variables of sectarian interests, some of them overlapping, others canceling out one another, I frankly could not advance any invulnerable reason for my preference for a solution that did not involve disintegration. I had been involved in discussions with countless numbers of people both before and during the crisis, mostly colleagues within the pro-democracy movement but also outsiders—businessmen, intellectuals, students, traders, professionals, clergymen. The mood, for many of them, was this: Let us prepare for the inevitable separation or, at best, the loosest arrangement possible, such as confederation. During the most violent day of the anti-Babangida riots, trapped within the tumult of thousands that submerged my car, sat, drummed, or danced on it, voices would ring out with shouts of "Lead us out of this mess called Nigeria!" "I am ready, recruit me. Let's go our own way." "Why should others hold us back? Those who want to be ruled by soldiers, let them go with them. We can make it on our own." And so on.

All highly emotive, born out of deep frustration, but one must be careful not to dismiss such voices as products of an abnormal moment, of a temporary phase. They were outbursts that conveyed a summation of positions argued in offices, marketplaces, bus stops, factories, palace courtyards and more secretive recesses of traditional enclaves, classrooms and debating halls. They were a continuation of discourses begun in 1960, and even long before then. We heard them during the various Leaders of Thought meetings after the countercoup of July 1966, we heard the then head of state, Yakubu Gowon, declare loud and clear that there was no longer any basis for Nigerian unity. We were deafened by the apotheosis of such sentiment in the roar of guns during the Biafran war. There are of course those dissenting biographers and historians, the Establishment record-keepers who insist on writing and speaking of Biafra in inverted commas, in a coy, sanctimonious denial of a reality. We should even encourage them to write it *B———ra* or invent any other childish contrivance, like a literary talisman programmed to create a lacuna in a history that dogs our conscience and collective memory; every day still reminds us that the factors that led to Biafra neither were ephemeral nor can be held to be permanently exorcised. And instead of such evasive or pious devices, it would serve us better to think instead of what mutual interests need to be emphasized, promoted, and packaged with all the skill of first-class salesmen, in order to ground our nationalist sentiments in something more durable. We shall dwell at length, in succeeding lectures, on what such interests consist of, the internal actualities and sine qua non of nation being.

For now, let us say just that, from those who cannot bear the thought of a trip to yet another consulate to those whose business interests would be jeopardized by a breakup of the present entity or those whose political ambitions require a large expanse to breathe in, not forgetting those for whom the continuance of the nation as a single entity means only the restoration of long-forfeited or disputed real estate (we shall come to such examples in a moment), even to incorrigible idealists who have clung to our sixties' dream of belonging to an unstoppable nation, rich in human and material resources, a nation endowed with a seeming gift of leadership, one whose citizens anywhere in the world would be revered, courted as plenipotentiaries in their own right, simply by the very possession of the Nigerian passport. . . . Yes, whatever the individual or group motivations or expectations that compel this bond in the occupants of a national space, let us cling to them by all means and lodge them in the collective pot. But the language of "non-negotiability" simply has to be abandoned. It must be consciously terminated for reasons that are quite simple to grasp but are unfortunately obscured to a majority because of its overpowering Sunday-school rhetoric. At heart, such language is subversive because it is designed to stop intelligent confrontation with the very issues whose resolution is essential to guarantee the emergence or continuity of such geographical spaces as true nations.

Take the military, who evince the readiest propensity for recourse to such rhetoric. With monotonous predictability, every military junta will be heard to declare its iron resolve to keep the nation together. Very good. But suppose every act of that same military in government can be proved to have headed the nation in the opposite direction? What price its commitment? All that is served by the chest-thumping rhetoric is the right of the military to do anything, adopt and execute any policy no matter where it leads. A bugle rouses the nation to its mission of keeping the nation together while a mailed fist and studded boot silence the protestations, the warnings that the acts of the military contradict its glorious aims. And the same confidence trick is employed by well-known tribal or religious atavists, consumed by sick ambition. They tie their opposition in a vicious knot by imbuing its call for equitable dealing with a threat of secession, thereby weakening their moral demands and winning undeserved concessions by default. The opposition retreats from its just demands in order to evade a tag that properly belongs to the demagogue. I have watched these tactics at work with such monotonous success that I can only marvel at the helplessness of the maligned opposition.

Those who are obsessed with power must never be underestimated in their Machiavellian capabilities. Let us spend a little time now on the elections of June 12, 1993, surely notorious to the entire listening and watching world, even the normally insular United States, thanks to the ubiquity of CNN, and thanks to the fact that those elections did take place before O. J. Simpson allegedly murdered his wife and her friend. Since that earthshaking event, however, I expect that there has been very little follow-up—all our own fault, since we have not yet, like the Hutu, slaughtered half a million of our own in a period of a mere three weeks. However, what is happening today is that the army and its handful of civilian cheerleaders and beneficiaries of the current policy continue to hamstring the civilian opposition by maintaining ad nauseam that a return to June 12 will lead to the nation's disintegration. But these men are no fools; they know very well that, without the actualization of the results of the presidential elections of June 12, 1993, it is 100 percent certain that there never again will be an acceptable election exercise in this country. Never was a situation more neatly made for army rule in perpetuity. An attempt at a new election is made; it results predictably in boycotts and chaos, and how does the military respond? "Fellow countrymen, it breaks our heart. We really want to return to the barracks but the country is about to fall apart and we are sworn to defend the unified sovereignty of this nation. We shall announce a new transition program as soon as we've cleaned up some indiscipline here and corruption there. . . ." Such cynical, calculating double-talk! And the populace will, alas, continue to fall into such an obvious, emotive trap unless it first learns to banish that inviolability principle, unless it learns to respond in turn: Leave us to decide what is inviolable and what is not, and, for a start, the sovereignty of the expressed will of the people is number one on such a list. That remains the Inviolable of all Inviolables. Without it, there is no nation, only a military camp.

On our part, it is sufficient to state—not even to explain but simply to declare—our preference for continuing as one nation. And we must ground such a preference in self-interest, the common denominator, the common tangibly identifiable factor that governs the many choices that are agreed upon by society. We can then proceed to map out a strategy for removing all obstacles toward the realization of that common goal, the choice of remaining one, that we have acknowledged as the least problematic structure for guaranteeing our various areas of self-interest. But we must also not neglect to decide the precise nature of the *problématique:* That is, are we trying to keep Nigeria a nation? Or are we trying to make it one? The difference is crucial. It outlines the magnitude of the task and qualifies the methodology to be adopted. It returns us again and again to our commencing question:

When *is* a nation? That question, many would claim, is not a difficult question to answer in the case of our immediate contestant, Nigeria. For many, a "war of unification" or a "war against secession," followed by reconciliation, restoration, reconstruction, and all the other rs in the Hymnal of National Harmony, fulfills all the conditions of "when," which of course would make ours overqualified for the nation status. But we know it is not that simple, and anyway, who wants to go to war, if avoidable, simply to earn a certificate of nationhood? And war, needless to say, does not even guarantee the much-desired nation being. The Portuguese colonies, now sadly denationalized by internal strife—Angola and Mozambique especially—were more "nation" under Portuguese rule, that is, during the liberation struggle, than they are today. They built a nation right under the repressive structures of the Portuguese and in the throes of war. They had a government in place—a government of the bush, of rudimentary structures, health and educational programs, but a government just the same. A grassroots government whose revolutionary cadres moved with and were part of the fighting forces, setting up administrative structures as the land was progressively liberated. Southern Sudan does not appear to have succeeded as effectively as was the case in Guinea-Bissau, Angola, or Mozambique. This I do find regrettable, for the history, travails, and valor of these forgotten people demand that, if only in our conceptualizing, they attain the status of nationhood. The Sudanese government is a tyrannical imposition, no different in kind from those other colonizing powers from which we claim, boastfully today, to have freed ourselves.

But, as we have said, the route is not necessarily war. A people can proclaim their readiness to evolve into a single entity or make the quantum leap into such a status, confounding both their own scepticism and the expectations of external sceptics. A single act can constitute a sudden total transformation, although of course even this so-called quantum leap is a progression of several motions, setbacks included, and the companion changes in the psychology of the people. What happens is an unpredicted concertation of interests, a dramatic, usually emotive moment that brings with it an unprecedented resolve, often focused on a charismatic leadership. Sekou Toure's Guinea, at that moment of "*Non*" to the ultimatum of Charles de Gaulle, was a memorable instance of one such transformation. But it need not be that dramatic. That quantum leap, or rather that quasi-quantum leap, can be effected through the most mundane, unglamorous means. Such as the ballot box. And this was the case with Nigeria on June 12, 1993.

A lack of glamour, of bravura, does not denote a lack of the heroic will. The achievement of the Nigerian nation on that day was most certainly a feat of heroic dimensions. Let us always recall that restraint and self-control are not easy virtues, and these were palpably on display on that day, and not merely then, but in the months preceding. After the physical and moneyed thuggery and coercion of the party primaries, chastened by the contemptuous manipulations of a wily dictator, realizing so belatedly that they had been playing not their own game but a game set and disrupted at will by a wily, supposedly neutral referee, the dictator Ibrahim Babangida, the members of the political class and their followers woke up from their costly yet infantile games and settled for the one weapon that their real foe never believed that they did possess or could exercise: self-discipline!

All the auguries were contrary. Two presidential contenders, both Moslem, in a country that claims to be evenly split between Christianity and Islam. Then one contestant who also picked a Moslem as his running mate. And the rancor of the primaries, both those canceled and the one that eventually survived, was still deep. Even the horse trading that went into the choosing of running mates had left its scars, deep disaffection, and had even traumatized parts of the electorate. Yes, the auguries were very contrary. June is the wettest of months, possibly the running mate of July, yet the skies held back all over the country. Not one drop of rain was recorded anywhere, not even in the chronically lachrymose belts of the south, not one drop fell to disrupt orderly process in one polling booth. Despite evident gaps in preparation, since the dictator had no intention of relinquishing power and was prepared to cite a messy process as an excuse for postponement or cancelation, the electorate's will rose palpably to make up the difference. Volunteers, acting as a united bipartisan community, filled the gaps and policed their own stations.

No need for illegal or contestable improvisation was encountered anywhere; the structures of voting and counting were unimpaired. Order was the order of the day.

The rest is factual knowledge: the orderly completion of voting in all states, the orderly collation and attestation of results in all wards, local governments, senatorial districts and states . . . commencement of the announcement of results nationwide, state by state, then, suddenly, the pseudo-legal interdiction placed on the continuation of the broadcasting of results! The announcements were already halfway through when a midnight court was convened in Abuja at the instigation of the dictator, operating through one of his many errand-boys, the lickspittle Chief Arthur Nzeribe, after it had become obvious that the clear winner was Moshood Abiola and not his opponent, Bashir Tofa. Tofa, a straw figure specially set up by the perpetuation machinery of I. B. Babangida and Halilu Akilu, was, needless to remark, confidently expected to win. Even his "election" at the party primaries, virtually by acclamation, remained a nine-day wonder in a nation whose trademark is the ubiquity of negative miracles. Babangida required such a nonentity for his endgame; now he was left with nothing but options between the desperate and the fatal. He chose to put a legal face on his decision, using Nzeribe and his phantom "Association for Better Nigeria." On June 23, he took the final, fatal step and annulled the elections. Violent protestations from within, diplomatic warnings from without . . . rebellion among Babangida's own army chiefs . . . labor strikes . . . Finally the manipulator found himself outmaneuvered, cornered and disarmed. There was no other recourse but to crawl out of office, humiliated. Like the incorrigible spoiler he was, however, he first set up a puppet civilian president, unelected, to ensure that the winner, Moshood Abiola, would not succeed him. And of course, he needed to protect his back.

The very nature of Abiola's electoral victory, the achievement of the electoral event itself despite all obstacles placed in the way of the Nigerian electorate by the dictatorship, may enable one to understand why—to cite one instance—the normally forensic mind of one of our irrepressible tribe of democracy advocates, Gani Fawehinmi, winner of the 1993 Bruno Kreisky Human Rights Award, went suddenly metaphysical. Gani's elation was unreined; he declared that there was a mystic inevitability to this sequence of events, reinforced his conviction with a narration of the coincidence of certain figures, dates, and I forget what else— but all pointing to the conclusion that Babangida's disgrace was divinely ordered and that Moshood Abiola was a man long destined to become the new president of Nigeria. It was difficult not to be infected with such hyperbole. So extravagantly did the forces of benign augury first indulge, tease, bloat, fill with hubris, then move to rout and demolish the agents of negative prognosis, that one could hardly escape the notion of some kind of birth anguish. And if, at the time, one could not give a name to this abnormality, it certainly began to define itself as the results of the election rolled in and the nation knew that a miracle was taking place. A candidate was defeating his opponent in that opponent's own base, defeating him among his own clan, his own state and region. The enemies of this birth tried to wind the umbilical cord round its neck and stifle its birth cries, but it would not be silenced. They tried to present to the waiting populace a fetus from past labors, lamenting the stillbirth of such a long-awaited moment, but no one was fooled.

A Parenthesis in Dissent—and Deceit

Yet even this birth was flawed, a few voices dissented, flawed fatally, they insisted. One candidate was overwhelmingly elected from his own home base, the Western Region, which is the home of Abiola, a Yoruba, and this became the grouse of a select race of supranationalists, the most strident of whom was Chief Odumegwu Ojukwu—remember him?—the erstwhile leader of that same breakaway region that took the name of Biafra as its new nation identity and plunged the nation into civil war. There are far too many reasons why we dare not ignore the attempt by Nigeria's expired warlord to justify the travesty of an annulled election, so let us pause here a moment and probe the tissues of this weighty distraction.

I happen to be a Yoruba, from that region accurately and until recently described as the Western Region of Nigeria, but lately (since the elections) referred to as the southwest. It would not matter if the government propaganda network succeeds in persuading the world that the Yoruba occupy only a coastal reef off a south-southwest peninsula; the statistical reality is that the Yoruba form the largest single nationality within the Nigerian space and therefore constitute a significant force within the electorate. The southwest redefinition was of course only a transparent ploy to reduce the base of Moshood Abiola's first-line support and contract a nationwide outrage to a chauvinistic protest by a minuscule corner of the nation. Many Nigerian journals and public commentators—and the international media especially—are unaware, till today, that they have been slickly manipulated into adopting the reductive label and would be genuinely surprised at how recent it is. This west, however, is the region that is alleged to have committed this heinous crime of voting massively for its own "shon of de shoil."

Now, as it happens, I did not vote. I did not even register as a voter, since I had repudiated, frequently and publicly, the entire transition process from the moment that Babangida and his faceless experts wrote and presented the manifestoes for the two parties. I could live with the imposition of a two-party system, being a proponent of the position that the immediate post-military régime should be regarded as the real *transitional phase* to democracy, during which a Sovereign Nation Conference would review all the policies of national import inherited from successive military régimes. Till today, however, I remain astounded by the sheer effrontery of actually imposing political manifestoes on the two parties! Well, I did not vote but, again, as I have repeatedly observed, even those who refuse to exercise their electoral rights are committed by the results through the mere act of belonging within that polity. The results bind them, willy-nilly, unless they have the resources, the will, and the organization to overturn the entire proceedings by demonstrating its illegality. Now, I wish to declare that if I had voted, I would have registered what would have amounted to a negative vote in favor of the eventual winner, M. K. O. Abiola, that is, I would have registered a vote against his opponent, Bashir Tofa.

And the reason? My sense of democratic accreditation makes it impossible for me to vote for a candidate who first flew the kite for the perpetuation of the Babangida military dictatorship—at least until the year 2000, as Mr. Bashir Tofa proposed in 1990. Nothing, absolutely nothing, no inducement of any kind, no revelation of genius on any front could make me even consider a vote for someone who, to make matters worse, had not even himself written the article in question but merely fronted for that initiative of Halilu Akilu, the head of Nigeria's combined security services and—as I have described him in the preface to my instalmental biography, *Ibadan*—a singularly repellent and sadistic example of that species well observed by Charles Dickens, the Uriah Heeps of the world. We very easily and conclusively established that this sinister creature was the actual instigator of the article that appeared in the *Daily Times,* even as he was the main executor and co-architect of many other dictatorship self-perpetuation ploys.

Among several of such ploys was the misbegotten Association for Better Nigeria funded and controlled from Aso Rock, the seat of government, but fronted by the earlier-mentioned Chief Arthur Nzeribe, an "incontinent ponce of power," with the same mission of pleading with the dictatorship to prolong its stay in power for the good of the nation. The cynically named Association for Better Nigeria plagued the nation with full-page paid advertisements detailing the virtues of retaining Babangida in power and claimed to have a followership of twenty-seven million Nigerians, out of a total population of ninety million, of which half must be pronounced juveniles. One wonders where all twenty-seven million were hiding when fourteen million trooped out to vote on June 12, 1993.

If one may just fill out a little more the tapestry of the colorful dramatic personae, a veritable tapestry of rather unappetizing prostitutes, we are obliged to mention also Akilu's creation of the Council of Elder Statesmen, fronted this time by an ex-politician and ex–other things, S. Grace (Gomsuu) Ikoku, a self-pronounced socialist angel long fallen from grace. Overnight was its birth, and it expired, like certain species, I am told, of the butterfly or some other winged insect, after a single act of copulation that must be held to have taken place when the council was received in audience in Aso Rock. There it tendered a humble petition to Babangida to look favorably upon the suffering nation of Nigeria and ride on her back for a few more years. The likes of the Third Eye and the mystery Dr. Farouk, all avid correspondents, columnists, sponsors of full-page advertisements, litigants, and so on—without one exception, they were created from the desk of Halilu Akilu, in a permanently retained suite of the Nicon Noga Hotel, Abuja, in one of the inner chambers of Aso Rock where Chief Arthur Nzeribe was ever to be found making useful and preposterous suggestions, fomenting kidnapping schemes (on his own later encountered to set individuals within the opposition against one another. Their wives and families were not spared, but why go on with this sordid story!

Researchers in mass communication are guaranteed, I promise, one of the most fascinating fields of research in the plethora of mainstream, underground, fake underground, pseudo-mainstream, and so forth publications that stretched public credulity to the limit during this political phase of the Nigerian crises. Since I must, however, acknowledge my own share of the responsibility for goading the Nigerian media into the samizdat tradition—in public lectures, media workshops, and private discussions, as the logical response to the arbitrary closures of media houses—I can only shake my head in chagrin at the many faces worn by Esu,* unquestionably, in this context, the muse of poetic justice!

The Reversible Ikemba

Such were the last desperate days of Babangida in office, and such was the cause that at least a sprinkling of intellectuals, a predictable section of the political class, moldy call-me-comrade radicals of the mold of Uche Chukwumerije, and rehabilitated secessionists somehow found congenial to their individual ambitions. Since Biafra is a well-known subject in these parts, and the name, pate, and beard of Odumegwu Ojukwu, the leader of that breakaway enclave, did attain iconic dimensions in universal imagination, at par with the images of swollen kwashiorkor bellies of Biafran children, this recent history will be incomplete without tribute being paid to him for his role in these various

*The trickster deity, agent of reverses.

admission, but we know it went much further), proposing character assassination tracts, and collaborating in producing forged issues of the opposition press to confuse the public. Brand-new publications appeared overnight from nowhere, accepted in good faith by the brave, elusive band of street vendors, sizzling publications with edifying and invigorating titles such as *Blade,* the *Razor,* and *Skeleton.*

Hyperactive within this new industry was yet another mercenary, Chief Tola Adeniyi, specially appointed editor of the partly government-owned but totally government-controlled *Daily Times,* a notable habitué of these murky corners of power, far from his official desk in Lagos. His specialization was the fabrication, editing, and printing of the material for those maverick publications, an activity that he carried out on the machines of the *Daily Times.* After the fall of Babangida and his fallout with the forces of law and order, leading to investigation of embezzled funds, his house in Ijebu was searched and galley proofs of those titles were stumbled upon. One of them, my favorite, was already proofread, corrected, and ready for press. On its front page was the screaming headline WOLE SOYINKA IN SEX AND FRAUD SCANDAL. And a well-documented, well-researched exposé it certainly was, filled with signed depositions by all sorts of mysterious characters, with photostats of checks, invoices, receipts that would take a team of auditors and handwriting experts years to unscramble. We were familiar with these documents, the warmed-up, newly spiced confections of earlier, failed efforts at public embarrassment that had only landed their fronting author in both libel and criminal courts. In any case, I was in good company. The editors of opposition newspapers, who were professional colleagues of this shadowy character, Tola Adeniyi, fared much worse. Apart from their own share of these "well-authenticated" scandals, their names appeared on the masthead as editors and publishers of the scandal sheets—one of the crudest attempts I have ever machinations. I have already referred to the necessity of admitting into our nation calculus all significant elements of self-interest, then seeking a way to accommodate them in a practical way, abandoning all further pretense of idealism and "patriotic" fervor. Odumegwu Ojukwu, former head of state of the short-lived Biafran nation, is one unassailable instance of this hardheaded view of the patriotic instinct. The Biafran and Ojukwu's grip on the world's historical memory is so deep that even today, and indeed during any post-Biafran crisis, I find I am often asked this question: By the way, what has become of that Biafran man, you know, the one with the heavy beard and heavier Oxford accent?

The answer is relevant as ever, and in his own words, the title of the slim, near-barren exposition of such assiduously sought relevance, his biography, "Because I am involved." The nature of Ojukwu's involvement has taken many bizarre turns since his "triumphal" return to Nigeria in 1982, enticed thither by a desperate Shehu Shagari who was bent on wooing the Igbo (ex-Biafrans) into the folds of his party for his re-election campaign. To all Nigerians, and this includes a majority of his own Igbo people, Ojukwu has demonstrated a remarkable involvement with the project of browsing where the pasture appears greenest. Since first shocking the nation, except, it must be conceded, a handful of diehard followers, by pitching his camp with a party, several of whose leading figures were certainly culpable for the massacres perpetrated against his own people in 1966, a genocidal event that provided Ojukwu a moral platform for his secessionist gamble, Ojukwu's political career has been marked by a series of surprises. He holds, by the way, a chieftaincy title, the Ikemba of Nnewi, but many Nigerians find it more appropriate these days to refer to him as the Reversible Ikemba.

So, it was not really acting out of character when the Ikemba began a series of courtesy visits to Babangida to express solidarity with him and to salute his courage in canceling the 1993 elections. Upholding the results of the elections, he declared, would have plunged the country into chaos, for it would have signaled a return to ethnic politics. The Ikemba's voice was also to be heard on the BBC, hysterically expounding the same thesis, backed by a species of logical proceeding that was anchored, it would appear, on the fact that Moshood Abiola's own people, the Yoruba, voted en masse for him. Never a mention by the Ikemba that Abiola *also* defeated his opponent in his own home base or that he scored handsomely among Ojukwu's own Igbo people. But does any of this matter? Bashorun M. K. O. Abiola won unambiguously according to every rule prescribed by the National Electoral Commission. Perhaps Ojukwu's recovered patriotism is best understood by the fact that, in the midst of the post-annulment crisis, Ibrahim Babangida actually found time to perform a magnanimous act of redress for wrongs long committed against our ethnic champion. One of the very last acts of the outgoing dictator was to sign a decree, virtually on the eve of his departure from Aso Rock, restoring to Ojukwu the landed properties that he had somehow forfeited or had been acquired by the Lagos state after the civil war.

In fairness to our worthy successor to the now-forgotten Moise Tshombe of Katanga in the politics of secession, Ojukwu has endeavored to live down that sobriquet "Reversible" by continuing in his new career with a remarkable consistency. Having shared Babangida's Last Supper, he ensured that he was virtually the first breakfast companion of Babangida's successor, the puppet Chief Ernest Sonekan, and was shortly after espied picking his teeth after lunch with Abacha, who had unceremoniously booted out Chief Sonekan after only four months in office. I believe that certain legal dots and dashes had been overlooked in the certificate of reoccupancy, thanks to Babangida's rushed exit from office.

However, we must not dwell overlong on these gilded birds of passage of our ongoing history, fascinating though they are. A glance at the mildewed tapestry of the stubbornly unfinished nation edifice is necessary only because of one's encounter with those perennial questions "What happened?" "How come you people can never get it right?" "Why has this or that logical route or that obvious alliance of progressive forces not been effected?" The human factor, alas, is a ponderous and imponderable factor of history. And so, just to round off, in Ojukwu's own words, our proposition that the nation imperative in certain situations is no more than a recognition and attractive packaging of issues of self-interest both of influential individuals and significant groupings within a geographical space, shall we preserve in marble—hopefully as Ojukwu's and not the nation's epitaph—his memorable declaration from the sanctuary of Aso Rock, "I am prepared to fight another war if necessary, this time, to preserve the nation's integrity"? Such sublime heights of patriotic eloquence should serve to recall us to the fact that history is not as impersonal as the structuralists of that discipline try to pretend it is, but is often dependent on the cravings and fulfillment, or lack thereof, of the stomach, especially at its most revolutionary or patriotic clamor.

A Nation's Date with Destiny

To return to that twelfth of June, what the nation perceived was this: Despite the intervention of practiced, back-alley abortionists, there was a birth, a miracle birth, a birth that was overlong in gestation but one that rendered all its midwives, including even the detached and non-participating, ecstatic. And should it really be considered even worthy of note that the immediate family, then the extended, would jubilate far more fervently and possessively than the rest of the clan? If some elders in the Yoruba west, particularly the Obas and traditional thinkers, choose to describe it, to regard it as peculiarly theirs, as a triumph for the Yoruba race, they have only reacted precisely as others have done in the past, and will continue to react as long as there does exist a Nigeria of many nations, and one whose recent travails have only exposed what many have long suspected: that there actually exists a grouping that believes it is divinely endowed to rule the rest! If some among the Yoruba wish to take a special pride in lancing such a long-festering though hidden boil, there is nothing to be astonished at in this, and certainly it is hardly the place of the cheats, the hegemonic minority, to take them to task over their euphoria. Nothing can erase the basic quality of the event; this was a *national* triumph, and the championing of its integrity must remain a national undertaking. If this achievement was abandoned by any, for whatever reason, let such falterers stay silent and stand aside, not add insult to injury with the self-serving ploy of assigning the tenacity of the rest to the fact that they happen to have been born in the south-southwest or on an island offshore of the southeast Nigerian coastline. For all those—no matter their place of origin—who have followed the events with amazement of eye and ear, who have marveled at the resilience of the people, their deft, assured motions to circum-vent both the mirages and the physical obstacles placed in the way of their self-determination by an illusionist who had run out of control, the savoring of this enormity of birth could not begin too soon nor could we hesitate any longer to give a name to the transcendental phenomenon of our times and our history. We understood then that the music of the spheres that presaged this event was in reality the annunciation of the birth of a nation.

So when the back-alley abortionists thump their khaki chests, and the thwarted hegemonists, bolstered by indigent but expec-tant warlords, join in the chorus of some risk to an inviolable nation being—through the actualization of the national will!—we can only ask, Who violated the nation being in the first place? When they declare that national oneness is not open to debate, we ask, Who was it that inaugurated the debate? If they still do not understand, let us remind them that it was they, the military and their handful of civilian traitors and turncoats, the Chukwumerije, the Akpangbo, the Sonekan, and their ilk, who laid the groundwork for the debate. I include those who, under the pretense that the integrity of the nation was higher than justice (as if the two values were in opposition!), proceeded to undermine the new birth by force-feeding it with a noxious interim broth—served by the wet nurse Ernest Sonekan—while they busied themselves with schemes for their own political ambitions, abandoning a sturdy but unweaned infant for an effete changeling that was neither fish nor meat, could not be described as animal, mineral, or vegetable. And with an ever-accelerating momentum, as the Chief Abortionist Babangida spread out his (the nation's) largesse and prospects of private prosperities with reckless abandon, even the midwives switched their adoration over to this changeling. Drowning their early cries of "Welcome the newborn and rededicate this cradle of birth," a new tune emerged, and it was not the Nigerian *national* anthem.

From one forum after the other, spearheaded by the Adamu Ciroma, the Yar'Adua, the Maitama Sule, the Sultan of Sokoto (the President-General of the Supreme Council for Islamic Affairs in Nigeria)*—who had earlier copiously cited the Koran to admonish Babangida for his reluctance to swear in the winner—all redesignated the compass of their Mecca and turned apostate within the very plenum of contemporary history. That is their privilege and their destiny. Where history must defend its own is against attempts to suggest that because the bastion of resistance is to be found within this or that region, therefore that region is

*See Appendix I for the text of the Sultan's press statement.

only motivated by ethnic considerations. Such attempted blackmail is not only unworthy of the proponents, it demeans the nation. If one single town, one village, one hamlet, one hovel is left that does, against all inducement, uphold a mandate that the nation has freely given, a mandate that others have equally upheld but have now chosen to abandon, then shame and dishonor belong to the side that has abandoned the struggle, and thus called in question once again, a nation question that was resolved on June 12, 1993. It truly saddens one to read the self-serving whine "Oh, we thought that it was a national struggle, but the Yoruba have turned it into an ethnic thing." The absurdity of this evident alibi for inaction, even betrayal, would be laughable except that it was cited by a number of ambassadors in reports to their home governments, providing such governments with a rationalization of decisions that lent a veneer of righteousness to an act of rape committed against the Nigerian nation. Only one section of the country is screaming "Rape!" ran the argument, so we need not lose a moment of sleep. The foreign television media—the VOA, BBC, Deutsche Welle, et cetera—as well as their print media appeared to take a peculiar delight in emphasizing what, in fairness, was indeed an observable fact: Protest was most intense in that part of the nation from which the president-elect had emerged. In the process, however, they deliberately ignored the historic fact that that same west has always been the spearhead of nationalist struggle, from colonial times, that the west was "where the action was," even though of course the dramatis personae of such struggles embraced, as they did in this instance, indigenes of every corner of the nation. In the process, they superficially attenuated the fundamental issue, which was centered on a *national* candidate and a *national* election, and that any rape of democracy is a violation of the claims of national integrity.

Not that the rest of the nation turned its back on the struggle, but for those who did, citing this fiction of the sectionalization of a collective enterprise, permit me to repeat a soccer analogy that I employed in a version of this same essay delivered as a public lecture in Nigeria. It has since acquired an unexpected poignancy, because it referred in a bantering tone to a Nigerian writer who at the time was undergoing nothing worse than the normal travails of a political activist, agitating on behalf of his own people, in this instance the Ogoni. Since then, of course, his situation has taken an ominous turn as, even as I speak, he finds himself on trial for his life. The other unexpected irony is that since that earlier lecture, this frivolously intended soccer analogy recently took on a prophetic life of its own, a larger-than-life contestation that I shall develop as a nation metaphor in one of my later lectures.

My remarks went thus: "I ask you to imagine a soccer team selected to represent the nation at a World Cup tournament. All soccer lovers, and by that I mean all lovers of the skills and dexterity displayed by the genius of soccer players, will agree that soccer or any game of skill should not be subjected to the idiocies of geographical representation, or to use that much discreditable expression, the harbinger of failure in any national undertaking, the 'quota system.' " To understand this peculiarly Nigerian-unity phrase, one has to conceive that the U.S. Olympic Committee or the government, instead of simply sending the "Dream Team" to Barcelona, insist on a team representation of all the states in the country. The supporting staff—coach, masseurs, counselors, government joyriders, security, and so on— would of course make up for the disparity between the number of actual players and the number of states. We continue,

Personally, I have never understood the phenomenon of fierce partisanship in competitive games, but I do concede that it appears that in every soccer lover, there is a nationalist totally out of control. So we imagine that we select a team that is predominantly Ogoni. Or better still, that there is an

Ogoni team that has whipped all other soccer teams in the nation, whipped all African teams, and performed so integrally as a team that soccer sense dictates that they go out to represent the nation in the World Cup. Lo and behold, they win, then get disqualified on a technicality that is open to contestation. At the very fore, the first to cry "Foul" and sustain his protest with unrelenting stridency will, in all likelihood, be Ken Saro-Wiwa, or maybe a royal father of Ogoniland. Saro-Wiwa sends a protest to the Federation of International Football [Soccer] Associations (FIFA) and the United Nations. His telex probably reads, "When will this international conspiracy against the Ogoni people end? First, your oil companies pollute our land and take our oil without compensation, now you conspire to cheat us out of our soccer victory!"

The royal father of Ogoniland puts on his best finery, calls a press conference, and demands to know why "our sons, our children," should be treated so shabbily. Now, ask yourselves how petulant, how infantile and incomprehensible as a soccer nation we would appear in the eyes of the world if the rest of the nation were to fold its arms, grumbling, "Well, see? There we all were, thinking that this was a national issue, but the Ogoni people have Ogonized it, so who are we to agonize!"

I little thought, as my audience responded soberly to those words in June 1994, months after General Sani Abacha had shown his hand, booted out the lame-duck interim régime of Ernest Sonekan, that the struggle of Ken Saro-Wiwa's Ogoni people for social justice would shortly reach that bleak phase where Ogoniland would be totally invested by a murderous "pacification" team sent hither by Sani Abacha. Neither did I foresee that we would be embroiled with FIFA in an all-out struggle to ensure that the junior version of the world soccer tournament was not permitted to grace Nigerian soil as long as Sani Abacha was in power and the president-elect, a man named by the Organization of African Unity (OAU) "African Pillar of Sports," was held in jail. All that would come later. My concern then, and till now, was to wean the political class, intellectuals, workers, and professionals away from their shameful sophistry, saying to them the following: If our hands were once laid in relay or in tandem upon the tiller, and your hand falters, weakens, or drops off finally, and you leap off the craft to the safety of the shore, do not invite the rest to abandon ship, whether doomed to sink or capable of salvage, and most definitely do not add an attempt to glorify desertion by dishonoring the resolve of the rest with the accident of their birth.

Needless to say, I had a few words also for the military, whose figurehead, Sani Abacha, had commenced all over again the transition game that had been so thoroughly discredited by his predecessor, General Ibrahim Babangida. Sani Abacha, it was clear from the beginning, had no intention of redressing the crime of his mentor and collaborator against the Nigerian people. On the contrary, he was setting himself up for an indefinite stay. In true mimic fashion, he had also taken on himself the task of fashioning a new constitution for Nigeria as a starting point for his own sequence of expensive diversions while he consolidated his hold on power. I hesitate to use my exact words as, outside the actual Nigerian situation, they sound, even to me, somewhat on the side of the "robust," so I shall situate them as an appendix for those who are truly curious to obtain a flavor of the nation's mood in those times (see p. 159). However, these were issues of life and death, situations that remain alien to many, and unreal even to others after the event, those who were potential actors and even victims at the time. I can think of no other way of conveying something of the authentic flavor of that very real, fatalistic mood of crisis when a handful of individuals accepted and acted with a hovering intimation that this might be their final contribution to a lifelong struggle than to cite a simple statement that dropped from the lips of Tai Solarin, an educationist, a septuagenarian, combative to the very end of his life, who was deservedly named "conscience of the nation."

The occasion was the ten-kilometer (six-mile) march from Idi-Oro, headquarters of the Nigerian Labor Congress, to the race-course in Lagos, on July 30, 1994. This was the last day of a two-week celebration of my sixtieth birthday organized "over my dead body" by stubborn friends. I had refused to participate in most of the events (there was nothing whatever in that nation to celebrate, this was my candid feeling) but decided somewhere along the way to stage a protest walk against the dictatorship as the finale of the fortnight's events, accompanied by pro-democracy activists. We advertised it as a "Walk for Justice," and it was in fact a probe toward the major march then under nationwide organization—the march on Abuja that I had first threatened on Martin Luther King's Day on January 15 that same year. I could not believe my eyes when I saw Tai Solarin appear in his accustomed combat khaki shirt, shorts, and hat. He looked ill, and I was quite distressed that this call had reached out yet again to his responsive spirit.

"What on earth are you doing here?" I demanded of his frail figure, all set to start with us at the railway crossing, sur-rounded and crisscrossed by scores of armed mobile police (we call them Kill-and-Go) in their armored vehicles and with crack-ling walkie-talkies. They had been ordered to prevent the walk, but an account of that morning's skirmishes belongs in another place. "There was no need for you to come," I persisted, looking at his wife, Sheila, for support—a waste of time, of course. She was every bit as feisty as her spouse. "Ah, Wole," replied the ancient spirit, "I thought I would come and walk a step or two with you."

Tai Solarin walked the entire distance with a small group, at his own measured pace, hailed by crowds as he passed, some of whom fell in step with him over different sections. He was accompanied by, separated from, then reunited with Sheila, as Abacha's goons hauled off the old man and his wife in separate wagons to nearby police stations, only to be compelled by besieging crowds to release and return them exactly where they had picked them up. They offered to give him a ride to the march's destination, but Tai was resolved to go out on his feet. Tai Solarin's "step or two" took him all the way to the rendezvous on Lagos Island, but he had a much further destination at hand, and I insist to myself till this day that I read it in his eyes that dawn. The following morning, he took the final step going up the stairs in his Sagamu home, missed it, and fell backwards to his death.

"A Step or Two with You" (Postscript)

We were confronted, still are, by a dictatorship specimen that was unprecedented in our experience of military viciousness. Under Abacha's direct command, over two hundred peaceful demonstrators had been mown down in cold blood on the streets of Lagos. I was present at one of the scenes of slaughter—the Ipaja area, June 27, 1993. The following exhortation should therefore be heard as part of and expression of the motions that involved multiple layers of resistance, from labor unions and professional organizations to traditional cultic resistance, one that involved the nocturnal placement of sacrifices at crossroads, invocation of ancestral curses on the enemy, distribution of *akara* offering to the deities, all the way through to the proliferation of cassette recordings of imprecational lyrics that had the police stymied: Just under what law do you arrest and prosecute a recording artist who predicts infernal tortures for a dictator that persists in thwarting the will of the people? Still, they arrested all they could, charged some to court, and mollified the beast of power.

The march on Aso Rock, seat of Abacha's government, was therefore intended to harness these already-existing forces of resistance, and expose, through sheer numbers, the emptiness of the claims of this latest protagonist of the military mandate. Since it was this threatened march that provoked, for the most part (to judge from our inside reports), the state measures that led eventually to my unorthodox means of exit from the country, it is a pertinent footnote to attach to an account of a nation's struggle to retrieve itself, both on the mental and the physical plane. That thwarted march will yet take place, but it will no longer be the peaceful march we planned when, at the celebration of Martin Luther King's Day in a Benin stadium, I commenced a preparatory call that I would later flesh out even more concretely at a public lecture in Lagos, at the Institute of International Affairs, where that same ill-fated Ogoni analogy was made:

If any craft is holed beyond redemption, reduced to no other remedy than to be scuttled as must be all dangers to navigation, that craft is the military. This is no time for us to indulge in palliatives; you, the military, have been dishonored, and you must know that there is only one way to redeem yourselves. You have dared to take this nation for a ride to nowhere, and the craft has broken down in midstream. Your word is no longer to be believed; indeed, your word has lost all communication currency beyond that of deceit and self-serving. All expressions of intent that have been manufactured by you deserve to be placed on the index of censorship: "transition program," "learning process," "phase one, phase two . . . ," "phase infinity!" "democratic agenda," "national stability," "the politicians have learnt nothing," "nonnegotiable," "newbreed politics," "political clearance to contest," "no room for moneybags politics," et cetera. Your word has lost value, and you have given up a time-honored profession, soldiering, for what properly belongs to politicians and writers, phrase-mongering. Empty, duplicitous phrase-mongering, where every declaration of intent leads inexorably to the opposite in execution. Your word, in short, now means nothing. You have lost all credibility.

So how, ask yourselves now, how do you expect to be entrusted with yet another program toward a democratic culture? What makes you think you have the authority to dictate the pace for the umpteenth time, decide a date for your departure and the commencement of civilian politicking? Both from the nature of your profession and from your past record in this direction, you have nothing to teach anyone, except perhaps yourselves. So when, precisely, do you propose to commence your sorely needed "learning process"? And where? The nation is, however, not a laboratory for any armed dilettante. You know the various institutions that can recall you to your professional role in this society; make use of them. Take an indefinite sabbatical from these distracting and alienating flirtations with power. Recall yourselves to what you are and regain our respect, even admiration, for your calling. That calling, let me assist you, is not of power but of service.

No, you cannot dictate the pace, you cannot decide our destiny. You robbed this nation of its moment of nationhood, and your reasons were petty, self-serving, and self-belittling. There was, you will admit, a vaster distance between apartheid power and the South African majority than there is between the Nigerian military class and the Nigerian people. Reflect upon this fact, soberly, and then work out the implications. One such implication is this: You have even less cause than the apartheid mind to speak or act as masters and overlords among our kind. Another implication is that you should find it far easier to reintegrate yourselves into an egalitarian polity than the aberrant species bred by apartheid. Where, then, is your problem? Why do you drag your feet? Twenty-eight years you have been at it, yet when apartheid finally looked in the mirror of its destiny and took the first difficult step, it was all over in five years.

Is it really in all seriousness that you propose to call a Constitutional Conference whose decisions will be subject to your approval? A conference, one-third of whose delegates will consist of your own nominees? In any case, a conference to discuss what exactly? And what of the constitution that was fashioned by minds from the same population from which you must find the new race of constitutional masterminds? Where did you pick up this notion that what the nation needs is a new constitution, a new time-wasting, money-consuming exercise that solves nothing and illuminates not one single corner of our darkened existence? Committees. Commissions.

Expense account. Nicon Noga five-star hotel. Travel allowances. Displacement allowances. And of course time. Time wasted and time burnt, but for you, time gained. Even if one were tempted for one moment to take such a conference seriously, the very composition of your preparatory commission gave the game away. With only two or three much to be pitied exceptions, these are individuals who are best forgotten; indeed, the kindest attitude toward these discredited individuals is a collective national amnesia. But they know how to give the illusion of substance to the hollowness of their assignation. This nation took a step, barely a year ago, to relieve you definitively of this self-appointed overseer role. By now, we should have been engaged in a genuine national conference, under our own aegis, while the business of government proceeded in its normal way. Within such a conference, you, as an interest group, would have been duly represented. But no, this does not content you. You have taken upon yourself a task for which you are ill-fitted—the Armed Democratic Guide! As Bola Ige recently demanded, would you invite him, a lawyer, to come and organize a conference on mechanized warfare? Would the Association of Nigerian Authors presume to organize an army symposium on tactics in jungle warfare, then nominate one-third of its membership (or fellow travelers) as specialists?

The people have said "Enough," and just in case it has escaped you, the people have lost all fear. The mystique of arms has been broken, but do not imagine, nonetheless, that there will be a heedless rush against your thirsty bullets. Even before your last champion Ibrahim Babangida pronounced the dread words, we did acknowledge that you are "managers of violence." We insist simply, on our part, that we shall be managers of our future. We invite you to be part of that future, but only on terms mutually agreed in freedom and equality. This resumed march toward democracy aims at a destination that will endure; we aim to build a national psyche that will ignore you, hold you up to ridicule when next we hear the voice of yet another ambitious savior polluting the nation's airwaves with that familiar formula of doom "Fellow countrymen . . ."

To the Nigerian populace, I urge on you a readiness for sacrifice. Spend each day as if it is your last in liberty, persuaded that whenever you leave home, it may be awhile before you regain the security of familiar surrounds.

The road to the prisons is wide open; we must not be afraid to tread where Martin Luther King Jr. has trodden, where Nelson Mandela spent his most virile years. There is no terror in a place where Obafemi Awolowo passed years in meditation, a place that Salawa Gambo made her second home. J. S. Tarka, Tony Enahoro, Gani Fawehinmi, Pa Ajasin, Michael Imoudu . . . the list is endless. All have shown by their example that the prison is only one more space that serves our rites of passage. We shall be teargassed, clubbed senseless, and some may even lose their lives, but you know and I know that some kinds of existence are worse than death, and the economic reality alone within which we are forced to exist shames and dehumanizes us. The condition of enslavement to a class that is bereft of solutions, an incontinent, spendthrift, power-besotted class, a class that lacks the will, even the integrity, to embark upon policies for the amelioration of the parlous existence of multitudes that cushion their existence, a class that has raised corruption to Olympian heights and made a sacred duty of deceit, imposes on us no other course but that of our own rescue mission. Are we such fools as to believe that if the results of what is probably the most laborious, most tortuous, most expensive elections in the history of the world are not implemented, an election that both we and the outside world declared free and fair, does anyone capable of serious thought really believe that if such a result is not made the basis of any political agenda in this country, there will ever be another election whose results will receive even a fraction of the acceptability of that last? It is time to commence a war of attrition against the class that bears responsibility for this undeserved hiatus in our progression toward nationhood. And if we must yet again sacrifice our present ease, our immediate self-fulfillment, so be it. But the beginning must be made *now!*

All symbols of military authority must be removed from our midst. Those arrogant photographs that desecrate public spaces, schools, hospitals, offices, even courts of justice. Street names, also, change them all. Remove them. Remove them by stealth, remove them openly, by cunning, remove them by bribery, remove them forcibly, remove them tactfully, use whatever method is appropriate, but remove them. I call on all who are resolved to play a role in our mutual liberation to participate in this exercise of psychological release, of mental cleansing and preparedness. Declare every day from now on a day of democratic sanitation. Later, in the quietude of a restored civilian norm, we shall assess which of them deserves to be honored, to be rewarded, even immortalized, and then we shall not hesitate to rename even my own Olumo rock after any such deserving uniformed servant of the people.

On January 15, 1994, on Martin Luther King's Day, in Benin, I insisted that the dreams of my generation on the threshold of our manhood were quite modest. Despite the constant companion shadow of despondency, we had, I suggested, trudged toward the fulfillment of those dreams for nearly four decades. In words that were adapted from Rosa Parks, the black seamstress of Montgomery, Alabama, who refused to move to a bus's back space reserved for the inferior race, I warned that "our feet are tired." And I described her plaint of exhaustion as a paradox, for what she was saying really was "I cannot budge. I will not budge." That seeming plaint was, in fact, a challenge, a summons. And a kindred spirit heard that cry in Selma and read its meaning aright, and his response was exactly in that same paradoxical vein, for what Martin Luther King said to the tired feet of all oppressed black people was "Let us march!"

So let us clean out our walking shoes, fill up our water bottles, fill our pockets with iron rations, and await the summons. The time is close, very close when, to retrieve our nationhood that was stolen by a directionless class, we shall march on Aso Rock!

The spoils of office, easy acquired taste

Distend the appetite, contract the scruples
A crow may answer eagle, perched on borrowed steeples

But crowns are crowns. When rulers meet, their embraces
Are of presence. Absent cries make empty phrases.

The Apotheosis of Master-Sergeant Doe

~~~~~~

The Spoils of Power:
The Buhari-Shagari Casebook

*T*his is a necessary interlude to provide pertinent space for the anecdotal material of history, far too often neglected. We are accustomed to the opening phrase in my verse epigraph given above—the spoils of office. The majority of a people of course belong to the "absent cries" that lack the crucial, recognized *presence* within whose aura the reality of the spoils of power resides. We must not commit the error of reducing their absence to mere physical terms, for there is nothing more debilitating to a people's psyche than the imitation of presence that we recognize in the condition of the internally exiled, muzzled like a dog, incapable even of howling "Intruder!"

For the moment, however, it is not even the absence or presence of the community of dissent, or deprived, in whatever mode, that concerns us. Nor is it, in this peculiar context, the spoils of *office,* no! It is that far more lethal, far less understood axis of *power* around which the history of a people often spins. The spoils that accompany power are not often recognized because they are not as particularized as those of office, but they nonetheless constitute a brutal exaction from a populace, savaging their psyche and intimating to them a kind of essential worthlessness. Perhaps other nations exemplify this as blatantly as Nigeria; beyond acknowledged Mafia-controlled societies, I know of none.

To obtain a basic understanding of today's reality of Nigerian politics, one had better learn about and come to grasp with the phenomenon of the spoils of power. Both quantitatively and qualitatively, in aspects of tenacity and duration, of manipulations of interest groups and the scale of attendant corruption, which is usually understood by such groups as patronage, the spoils of power continue to take central place in the various internal confrontations that have wracked that uneasy entity, Nigeria, since its fabrication by the British colonial power in 1914. This history is tortuous only because its major protagonists are schooled in the arts of political deviousness sustained by a Mafia-like operational strategy. For a long time, this center of intrigue has tended to deny its existence, a pose that was most favorable to the strategy of protesting adherence to an equal communality of interests while simultaneously pursuing the accumulation and perpetuation of power and its spoils. Today, faced with increasing proof, of sustained revelations of their narrow, bigoted, and hegemonic agenda, the upholders of this credo have gone on the offensive, proposing a most bewildering array of reasons why they are the chosen, why power is divinely, preternaturally lodged within their enclave. Forced out in the open to admit, with increasing arrogance, this mission that was originally bequeathed to them by the departing British colonial

masters but one they have adopted with relish, they have embarked on a program of political vengeance. This takes various
forms, on various levels of intensity.

But why revenge as response? The answer is ironic but logical:
It is simply revenge for being found out. Revenge for the personal and institutional inadequacies of the flag bearers of a self-
perpetuating ruling clique, unambiguously and repeatedly exposed. Revenge for their ineptitude and failures in governance,
which then tend to reflect unfavorably on the group's elitist
conditioning, thanks to the accumulated privilege of nearly
thirty years of occupying the seat of power since a nation's
independence. Revenge on the critical perceptiveness of the
ruled, who reject the actuality of social retardation that continues to be their portion. Revenge most bitterly exacted,
however—to return to the starting point—revenge for the exposure of that prolonged conspiracy to ensure that even if circumstances compel such an oligarchy to accept the proverbial
scraping of the barrel, to present as its current military or civilian
champion and flag bearer of its power mandate a certifiable
cretin, a drooling imbecile, a notorious drug baron or homicidal
maniac, no matter what, all resources, including human suscep-
tibilities such as religious incitement and its expenditure of
human lives, all, all must be mobilized to ensure that power
never drifts across a calculating divide that was inserted in the
map of Nigeria by the departing British colonial.

The problem of course is simply this: The enthronement
of power as the birthright of a given sector of any human
community evolves, sooner or later, into a privilege of medi-
ocrity, and logically still, into the quest for power, by right, on
the part of the mediocre. In the end, even the mentally deficient
grasps the real possibility—indeed, the absolute certitude—that
his turn has come. Understanding of the accessibility of power
and the means to it is not necessarily qualified by access to basic

intelligence; observation and cunning are quite sufficient, especially where the opportunity is spread over a long period of closeness. In short, what would take the average intelligence a week or less to grasp and execute or reject will require in the mediocre years of sporadic penetration, a painstaking accumulation of significations that persuade him, in the end, that he is every bit as qualified as his predecessors for the trophy of power. The faculty of waiting has become second nature because he knows no other way of existence. If, as in the Nigerian instance, he has grown to recognize a politics of revenge as practiced by his assiduous mentors, he grasps, in the narrowest sense, that this is what power means and wonders why he has been denied such a compatible commodity for so long. General Buhari, villainous despot as he was, was quite intelligent, but we all know that he could have been unseated by an illiterate sergeant major or corporal if the latter was able to grasp the essence of brutality and revenge. The signposting is now unmistakable: Those who fostered the politics of revenge are doomed to be consumed in turn by the Frankenstein they have unleashed. For now, however, they gloat over the fact that the immediate principal victims are from the south, and they goad on the monster, pointing out areas of neglect in which his instinctual propensities may be gratified.

No one, be that person a Nigerian or an alien visiting from outer space, no one, I am convinced, can proffer a more plausible explanation for the heedless assaults that have been mounted in recent times under General Sani Abacha against selective national figures in the south of the country, assaults that exceed even the worst inhumanities that were unleashed on the nation by Ibrahim Babangida in his final, desperate years or by that hypocritical, self-proclaimed salvationist duo, Muhamadu Buhari and Tunde Idiagbon (1983–1985), or indeed the state atrocities of the last desperate years of the civilian régime of Shehu Shagari.

We must expand these personalities a little in order to make sense of what they have made of the nation. Or more to the point, in order to understand how the nation came to take on the personality it has, for when a nation cannot be defined by an ideal, a purpose or direction, it becomes nothing but a cameo of personalities, a series of transparencies of distortion, each laid over the last. Two of these characters and their spawns are of particular interest to me in the present context, largely because of what they so glaringly represent in the province of the spoils of power. Also, we need to recall this past, the pattern of its political contests especially, in order to place in the appropriate context the events of June 12, 1993, to understand why the annulment of the elections of that day was not just another "unfortunate episode" in the checkered history of a nation but a dagger in its very heart.

The "Democratic" as Poli-Thug State

Shehu Shagari—to begin with that "quiet, unassuming, committed democrat" (as he appeared to Western powers)—was the civilian president who sowed the seeds of Nigeria's present bankruptcy through a party patronage economic policy known as the "import license" scheme. More to the point, for now, he also turned Nigeria into a police state as the countdown toward the 1983 election began in earnest, and he found himself compelled to read the cheerless writing on the wall. The desperate incumbent, the erstwhile humble, reluctant president, progressively sprouted claws and turned the nation over to the tender mercies of an uncouth, power-crazed police chief, one Sunday Adewusi, who promptly inaugurated a scorched-earth policy in order to ensure his master's second tenure as Nigeria's head of state. The Nigerian collective memory tends to be short, but there are many whose memories remain forever seared by the strutting appearances of the gross figure of Sunday Adewusi on television, flanked or backed by specially selected specimens of his uniformed killers. This inspector general of the Nigerian police would point to them and boast: "These men are trained to kill. Those who want to make trouble for this government will have to face them. I guarantee such dissidents the bloodiest experience of their lives."

Ambassador Joseph Garba felt obliged to devote a few lines to this aberration in his recent work, "Fractured History":

> The upholders of law and order had themselves become corrupted by their involvement with the ruling party. Inspector-General Sunday Adewusi was said to have become so partisan that it seemed he did not recognize himself as a public servant paid with the tax-payers' money. His police force was regarded as an instrument of oppression, particularly the Mobile Force which in its unbridled and excessive actions had earned itself the dubious sobriquet of "Kill and Go."

I hope my good friend Joseph Garba will forgive me for citing his cautious (diplomatic) phrasing in a context that cannot permit of academic niceties. However, I was *there,* so I am in a position to assert that there was no "was said" about Sunday Adewusi, no "was regarded as" about his Kill-and-Go. I saw them kill and go, time and time again. And they were also good at watching others kill under orders.

Just one instance among a thousand others of that last specific refinement: We were witnesses of their ordered inaction in the heart of Ile-Ife in 1982 as six members of a rival party were set on fire in a minibus as they drove to join a political rally. The police, numbering over a hundred, sat on their hands in four open-sided vans, their rifles and teargas launchers between their legs. They watched, with emotions varying from impassivity to helpless horror, as thugs of the National Party of Nigeria, under the command of a psychopath who styled himself "007," ambushed the minibus, firing from windows, then hemmed in the bus and set it on fire, clubbing back the occupants as they tried to escape. I pursued the course of this daylight massacre back to its origin and planning and confronted the officers from Iyaganku head-quarters (Ibadan), who showed me signals from Lagos in advance of the massacre. One of them said bitterly, bringing out a bulging file: "I investigated this man ["007"] myself and I have given my superiors more than enough material to hang him for several murders and drug trafficking long before now. But he is well protected." He showed me photographs taken by his department of a grinning Shehu Shagari lighting a cigarette for one other audacious party thug who practically flung his leg over the thighs of the seated "God-fearing" democratic president.

The campaigners were doomed from the start. The incumbent governor, Chief Bola Ige, a long-standing friend, always stayed in my house on Ife campus whenever he came that way on his campaign trail. I sat with him as he had his breakfast, discussing the political situation, when a young party member came in to convey the latest intelligence report he had received. He won-dered if they should not call off the various rallies planned for that area. I listened to them as they made the decision to cancel one that had been scheduled for a remote village, while hanging on to the one in the heart of Ile-Ife, in the confidence that they had requested and had been promised a strong police presence. It was my first meeting with that young aspirant of no more than thirty-two, and the last time I would see him alive. He was burnt to death with others, a victim of orders that had come from the very highest quarters already privy to the plot, approving an impressive police presence at the rally but with strict instructions that under no condition were the police to act. Not one suspect was arrested.

Now the question is this: How did it come about that this gross object, Adewusi, actually escaped even the mildest censure when his boss, Shehu Shagari, was overthrown? To claim that he had openly abused his office is to be guilty also of a criminal abuse of euphemism. This police boss had been responsible for several homicides, had provided vehicles and armed police protection for the thugs of Shehu Shagari's party as they terrorized the nation. Led by their immediate master, an NPN governorship candidate, one such poli-thug team invaded the police headquarters at Iyaganku, Ibadan, the state capital of Oyo in the west, to compel the release of their members who had been arrested for vandalism and homicide. Even more notorious was the standoff in Enugu during the court hearing of an appeal by a defeated candidate. Two sets of police confronted each other outside the court premises: the police unit that was protecting the judicial proceeding versus the fully armed poli-thugs that had come to enforce a verdict in favor of the NPN candidate! The latter laid siege to the court with an ultimatum: Declare me the winner or you will not leave these premises alive. Judgement, I recall, was declared in his favor. Let us keep the contrasting conduct of the elections of June 12, 1993, constantly in mind as we sketch in a few more instructive details of this gladiatorial democracy from the past, a decade earlier.

These thugs traveled around in motorcades, led by police sirens! In the latest volume of my somewhat fictionalized memoirs, *Ibadan: The Penkelemes Years*, I recount the role of the police in escalating the tempo of violence—extra-judicial killings, torture, et cetera. Those who come across that account of political violence in the then Western Region of Nigeria in 1964 are invited to visualize a parallel scenario in 1982–1983, but this time on a scale of a hundred to one against that of 1964. Adewusi acted virtually as a member not only of Shehu Shagari's cabinet but of his party. He sat on deliberations of that party, entered his own nominations for cabinet positions and struck others off, shared openly in the looting of the nation's wealth, and sent in his fronts for political preferment.

In most coups d'état, especially those mounted by a genuinely corrective junta, the likes of Adewusi would normally be among the first to be lined up and publicly shot. Yet not only was this man Adewusi retired peacefully, but the Buhari junta announced, within a matter of weeks, certainly less than a month, that he had been retired with full benefits and that he had indeed collected all his gratuities and other entitlements. You need only contrast this with the present writer, who resigned from university teaching in Nigeria in 1985. I am supposed to be a university pensioner, but I assure you I have yet to collect one cent in gratuities, in pension or any other damned entitlement. Always one form missing or one piece of information incomplete. Inspector General of Police Adewusi cleared all those bureaucratic hurdles within a month and is to be found, even today, among the revered councils of advisers to successive governments!

I earlier posed this question: How does it come about that such unrepentant careers are hardly ever penalized and are even routinely rewarded? The answer, which we shall address as we proceed, goes to the heart of the malaise that is the lot of Nigeria at this moment and sums up the political futility of the present relationship between its parts, based on a jealous monopoly of the spoils of power. For now, let me just add that it was during the terror régime of Adewusi that the surrealist event took place that I recounted in the preface to a new edition of my prison memoirs, *The Man Died,* involving a medical doctor and colleague who was arrested for picking up some injured survivors of one of Adewusi's murderous assaults on unarmed citizens in Akure, a town in Ondo state. Even as his patients were bleeding to death in his station wagon, unattended, he was locked up, accused of being a doctor of rebels, and tortured. The ironic twist came when his torturer informed him, just as a "by the way," that he had once been a student of his victim in his university days. The very stuff of a playwright's improbable imagination, played out in the dingy cells of a rural town in western Nigeria!

Yet this took place during a supposedly democratically elected régime, a scenario that was played out over and over again in the months before and the months that followed an election so cynically rigged that a state governor, elected through that very process, went on television to declare openly what everyone knew, that his opponent was the actual winner. No, Dr. Victor Omololu Olunloyo, a mathematician turned politician, was not undergoing a crisis of conscience. It was more a crisis of finance. By the time he was moved to protest, it was over a month since his stolen tenure in office and, alas, no funds were yet forthcoming for the running of the state, much less to redeem political pledges. The federal treasury had been emptied in the prodigal and illegal use of resources to ensure the electoral victory of the National Party of Nigeria at the elections, so Shagari, back in office, could not meet his statutory allocations to the states. (On the road called "Road 9," which served as a back route between my university, Ife, and the township, there was a warehouse constantly filled to the ceiling with scarce and expensive consumer items—bags of rice, sugar, television sets, and so on—to reward the faithful, replenished on a daily basis by trailers from government warehouses in Lagos. When the insurrection began after the cynical victory of the NPN, the storage was festally illuminated in an unforgettable bonfire.) With the elections over and the government-in-party overspent, salaries could not be paid nor could public services be maintained. It was becoming difficult even to pay for the quantity of fuel that was consumed by the police motorcade that accompanied His Excellency whenever he shuttled to and from Lagos in attempts to squeeze funds from Shehu Shagari.

It is difficult today, even for those who, like me, were in the thick of the fray and monitored its drain on the national treasury, to accept the level of callous depletion that was inflicted on a nation's resources. The NPN had, however, sworn to astonish the nation with a "landslide, seaslide, moonslide" victory, and all the demons of hell were let loose to fulfill the galactic undertaking. One of the very finest that the U.S. university system ever produced, Dr. Walter Ofonagoro, had been recruited from his American base to nail this message on television—the NTA, a nationwide and state-owned station—onto the stubborn heads of the unconverted. His nightly program, *Verdict 83,* hurled imprecations on all opposition from a uniquely askew but cavernous orifice, an inundating spittle-launcher situated somewhere in his head. Watching his nightly performance as one does, in perverse fascination, a spitting cobra, I could not help recalling a Walter Ofonagoro whom I had encountered at a university in New York during my itinerant lecturing rounds. His arm was then in plaster, broken in several places by some students who, according to his version, felt that he had graded them unfairly in their exams. They had apparently waylaid and set on him with baseball bats. I was naturally indignant and sympathetic at the time, but now I am convinced that his version of the story calls for careful investigation. If true, severe sanctions against those students—if the statute of limitation offers them no protection—should be invoked for botching a chance to do Nigeria a terminal favor. That Dr. *Verdict 83* should surface yet again as General Sani Abacha's megaphone is merely the crowning glory of the career of a decadent and prurient intellect that constantly finds a congenial spot in the service of imbeciles.

The cost of recruiting U.S.-trained "experts," however, formed only a minuscule, indeed inconsequential drop in the ocean of waste that was the consequence of breaching the dam of a national treasury to irrigate the insatiable gorge of the party coffers. Elections were now over, the NPN had sworn itself back into power, but the nation's financial situation had become so desperate that virtually the first task that Shagari's government assigned itself was to negotiate a loan from the World Bank. By then, once again, I found myself obliged to leave the country. No, that is not quite accurate; I was virtually bundled into a plane by the very police killers who had been sent after me ("We can't protect you any longer," they said, "others are bound to get you"). I tried to spend those three months away usefully, campaigning in Europe and the United States against that loan, wrote Op-Ed pieces for the *New York Times* and other newspapers denouncing the elections and the reign of a police state. I warned that the loan was sought purely for sharing among the party leaders whose pockets had been drained by the election campaign. Against the tide of laudations by Western powers on the democratic victory of Shehu Shagari and media claims of a nationwide acceptance of the elections, I wrote articles predicting that the term of Shagari's régime would be one of the shortest ever, that its existence would be curtailed either by public insurrection (preferably) or by a military coup. For my pains (the NPN needed that infusion of cash as helplessly as a heroin addict needs his shot), yet another squad was sent to stop me, and I had to keep moving—France, Germany, United States—anywhere but London, where Adewusi's killer squads were most solidly entrenched. These personal details are, excusably I trust, inserted from time to time purely to remind ourselves that these were no abstract games in a political tussle, but that conspiracies to drain away the lifeblood of a nation are never without corresponding schemes for the elimination of real or imagined obstacles. Also to recall the fact that, in the elections of June 12, 1993, there was no reported activity of voluntary or involuntary exile from any Nigerian until Ibrahim Babangida intervened to annul a peacefully conducted election.

That, in short, was the level of the financial crunch experienced nationwide, and this included even those who, like Olunloyo, were rigged into office by the NPN's murderous machinery. And thus it came about that His Excellency was obliged to appear on his state television to address his subjects on why government was at a standstill and expectations from electoral promise still unfulfilled; it was not his fault, he explained, there was simply nothing coming from the center despite promises and statutory obligations. And, speaking directly to his boss in Lagos, he warned that if such funds were not forthcoming, and soon, he would quit office and turn the government over to his opponent who, after all, he declared, was the rightfully elected governor.

Such were the obscenities and arrogance of power to which Nigerians were treated during the incontinent reign of the National Party of Nigeria, led by Shehu Shagari, until it was abruptly terminated four months into its second mandate by the supposedly ascetic team of General Buhari and Tunde Idiagbon. A corrective régime declared a manifesto that made Cromwell's puritanic agenda read like a day in the life of Sodom and Gomorrah. So, how did they proceed to fulfill this project of national redemption?

Because of its exposure of the universe that often separates the world of declaration of intent from that of action, I shall mostly utilize the unprecedented mode of the Shagari-Buhari interplay as elaboration on the theme of the spoils of power. However, we must also cast more than a glance, as we have already begun to do, at some of the other runners in the power relay, since, in one of the attempts to resolve the present crisis, calls have been made in some quarters to invite them back—Shagari and all—as a kind of interim governing team of elder statesmen whose wisdom and experience would ensure a return to democratic sanity. It would appear that such would-be arbiters of discord have never heard the story of the "mousing emir."

When pressured by the British colonial administrator to put an end to his slave raids and stick to less-objectionable trading pursuits, the truly astonished man exclaimed, "Can you tell a cat to stop mousing? I shall die with a slave in my mouth!"

A "Dis'plinary" Cat among the Pigeons

The background to the Buhari intervention has already been provided, but let us quickly recapitulate:

Shagari's government was already in disfavor throughout the country. The arrogant corruption that turned Nigeria into an economic disaster zone had already eroded what little credibility it had in the nation. Under its four-year rule, Nigeria had, for the first time in her existence, begun to import basic food items. The import license scam that was used by the party as reward and enticement for party loyalists and would-be supporters cost the nation billions of dollars. A Presidential Task Force on Rice Importation, headed by Umaru Dikko, was responsible for yet more billions simply sucked into private accounts, while food production in the country virtually ceased. The highly publicized OPERATION FEED THE NATION campaigns proved to be nothing other than opportunities to again siphon the country's resources into private pockets through massive importation of fertilizers and publicity campaigns that were totally unattuned to the farmers' needs or farming culture. They existed only for the jobs that they provided to poster printers, motor dealers (for fleets of vehicles), traveling and hotel expenses for the bureaucrats. In my hunting excursions, I would come upon a few symbolic bags of fertilizers simply tossed on the pathway and abandoned, having been "distributed" by party contractors to the satisfaction of pay offices. The local farmers to whom I spoke neither knew how they got there nor who owned them. The national debt had spiraled out of control, and even the businessmen and entrepreneurs who were traditional supporters of the NPN, with its blatantly capitalist orientation, had become aware that their own interest was threatened by a régime of unprecedented incompetence and indifference.

By the 1983 election, most of the avenues for siphoning money from government coffers had become atrophied for lack of content at the source. A nation of high expectations had become a beggar nation, a laughingstock in the financial centers of the world, but still indulged by the same commercial interests and their governments, buoyed by the knowledge of the "black gold" that lay extensively beneath its soil. Finally, insurrection had raised its bloody head in many states.

Together with his iron-faced right-hand man, Idiagbon, the willowy, seven-foot-plus general, Buhari formed a duo that earned a reputation as exceptions to the rule of corruption and other rulership vices. The sociology of this period would make for a dozen doctoral theses. Discipline, or rather "dis'plin," was their slogan, and this was to be manifested in all sorts of public motions, such as inculcating the culture of queuing; patriotism, which mandated flying the national flag even on roadside shacks that sold nothing but oranges and peanuts; sanitation, cleaning up the environment; fiscal control (you went to jail if you forgot some loose foreign coins in your pocket and failed to declare them at the airport) . . . and so on. They introduced a compulsory Sanitation Day, every last Saturday of each month from dawn until noon, when the entire nation was expected to stay at home and clean up the environment. Only essential vehicles were permitted on the roads. Defaulters were detained at roadblocks mounted by excitable sanitation squads supervised by military officers or police. Their notion of "dis'plin" was not to take offenders to the local magistrate court or even sanitation tribunals but to make them do the frog-jump. For the uninitiated, this exercise requires that you attach your hands to both ears while you jump up and down in a squatting position.

The same pattern of humiliation was inflicted on civil servants, both junior and senior, who reported late for work in their offices. The state governor would arrive at some government office a few minutes before clocking-in time, wait until the clock read half past seven in the morning precisely, then lock the gates. Outside, his soldiers waited to drill and frog-jump all latecomers irrespective of rank or age. A few suffered fatal heart attacks from the unaccustomed exercise and others were hospitalized. The nature of their responsibilities was irrelevant. Anyone acquainted with the variety of public responsibilities knows that, in the course of some duties, an officer may not be expected at his desk until later in the day and sometimes not at all, since he might be in other, related offices carrying out inspections, auditing, or simply holding scheduled meetings. No, none of that mattered, no explanation was tolerated. Dis'plin was dis'plin, and dis'plin meant being at your allocated desk at the appointed hour.

Let me confess here that, at such times, I greatly feared for my own people, feared for their measure and defense of self-worth. To understand the depths of such—yes—despair, you have to imagine the elderly gentleman who cleans the offices at Harvard University's DuBois Center being frog-jumped by a college law enforcement officer because President Clinton had declared war on public slackness. You must imagine such a slacker, real or imagined, being forced to undergo a military drill in the open street before students whom he could easily have grandfathered. You must also imagine him submitting to this assault on his dignity, on his humanity, with an ingratiating "Yes, massa" grin! Since I am familiar with the history of "dis'plin" meted out to plantation slaves for major and petty infractions, the sight of my groveling compatriots, such instant "Uncle Toms," could only make me wonder if it wasn't much easier than one would normally think to enslave whole peoples and make them grin and bear every form of humiliation. Once again, one awaits an in-depth sociological study of this truly troubling phenomenon.

There were of course exceptions. Some turned their backs on the dis'plinary squads, returned home, and wrote out their resignations. That was not always as easy as it sounds, as they were often horsewhipped on the spot or bundled into Land-Rovers and taken into barracks for further punishment. The horsewhip became the symbol of the times (hardly any uniformed man was to be seen without it) but of course the tradition began much earlier, rising into prominence under the brief tenure of General Murtala Mohammed, who, it is sometimes forgotten, made the first attempt to introduce a disciplined existence into a chaotic nation. Those who are interested may refer to my play *Opera Wonyosi* for my reaction to this trend at the time.

Buhari and Idiagbon, however, carried this to sadistic levels, glorying in the humiliation of a people in an exercise that was remarkable for its selectively regional application; let us keep in mind what I have referred to as the politics of revenge. Their motives were patently impure. It is true that today some Nigerians look on this period with some nostalgia, preferring it to the laissez-faire approach of Ibrahim Babangida, who was quite comfortable with external decay that was, after all, an outer reflection of the inner condition of his person and of his régime. Not a few Nigerians understandably look back with longing to that period when Nigerians were actually made to form lines at bus stops and public offices, when mounds of garbage did not substitute for city landscaping and there was actually a competitive pride in a hy-gienic environment. Let us face it, as many Nigerians themselves and visitors to Nigeria do concede, Nigerians appear at times to re-quire a coercive hand in directing their social awareness. There is something about my fellow nationals that requires that their sense of egoistic mindlessness be drastically pruned, that they be made to recognize the rights of others. As a former and still enthusiastic enforcer of road safety culture in Nigeria, I not only testify to this but confess that I took particular satisfaction in training our corps to crush the egos of that arrogant breed of drivers, the civilian elite and military officers especially, who felt that they were above the law and could kill and maim with impunity.

While on the subject of extracurricular activities indulged in periodically by this speaker, let me use one to emphasize the palpable visibility of squalor and depravity into which the country had sunk during the Shagaritic era. There are, you know, all kinds of Nobel laureates, many of them, especially in the sciences, justly famous for earthshaking achievements. Well, let them all solve the riddle of the universe, invent the transistor, break the DNA genetic code, find a permanent cure for AIDS. I bet none of them can boast of having actually made a record, which is what sets me apart from all the others! This activity was forced upon me by the level of moral, political, and environmental squalor of the Shagaritic era, and I devoted one stanza in that record, *Unlimited Liability Company,* to the physical aspect of this degeneration:

> The Russian astronauts flying in space
> Radioed a puzzle to their Moscow base
> They said, we're flying over Nigeria
> And we see high mountains in built-up area
> Right in the middle of heavy traffic
> Is this space madness, tell us quick?
> The strange report was fed to computers
> Which soon analysed the ponderous beauties
> The computer replied, now don't be snobbish
> You know it's a load of their national rubbish.

That the nation, beginning from the latter years of Ibrahim Babangida's era, has reverted to that pre-Buhari era may be recognized in the fact that I felt compelled to incorporate that song from *Unlimited Liability Company* into my recent play *The Beatification of Area Boy*.

I like to give the devil its due. Taking, for example, the boy scout dictator, Yakubu Gowon, who jailed me for over two years; I have gone on record to credit him with two achievements: (1) He opened up the country with a number of sturdy highways, and (2) he instituted the National Youth Service Corps, which was designed to foster a spirit of oneness among Nigerian youth. I regret to say that I have been unable to unearth one simple achievement that can be credited to Shagari's tenure, and thus Buhari may claim to have done the nation a favor by terminating the life of such a wastrel and unproductive régime. However, Shagari's greatest crime remains his attempt to subvert the very democratic processes that brought him into office and to turn the nation into a police (or poli-thug) state.

Shagari left a mess in every direction, a legacy of rot of which the rubbish heaps, mountains and mountains of them in the heart of the major cities, became a symbol. Buhari did wipe these out, with the same efficiency that he applied (with more than a little help from Brigadier Adekunle, the "Black Scorpion" of the civil war fame) in ending the career of the cement armada that choked up the ports of Lagos, earned enterprising foreign and local shipping companies—many of them formed for that very purpose—millions of dollars in demurrage fees, and contributed to an unimaginable extent in the bankrupting of the nation.

"Was This the Face That Launched a Thousand Ships?"

Let us spend a little time on this phenomenon that earned us such notoriety on the high seas, in shipping journals, in Lloyd's maritime insurance, and of course, throughout the world media. It became one of the sights that nearly begot a tourist trade; if Boston thinks that its 1992 flotilla spectacle of the tall ships was a tourist dream, I assure you that it was nothing beside the parade of vessels that stretched out from Lagos harbor into miles and miles of international waters.

Shagari's party men were ever full of ingenious ideas for spending Nigeria's money—that is, making a lot of Nigeria's money for themselves—and this was only one scheme out of a hundred or more, but one with truly spectacular results. They came up one brainstorming day with a nationwide federal housing project for low-income earners; it had the additional advantage of being such a populist, caring idea. This was, by the way, irregular, since housing on that scale properly belonged on the state list. To fulfill such an ambitious project, however, you do need a world of cement. The Nigerian cement factories could not, as the NPN knew, meet the requirements, so, of course, import! And did they import, utilizing the infamous import license scheme, which was the shortest cut ever devised for hemorrhaging a nation's foreign exchange reserves!

The news spread round the world: Shehu Shagari's régime needed cement, was paying for cement, would take in any amount, any grade of cement from anywhere. Letters of credit could be opened anywhere, by anyone, and the open-ended import license scheme was readily available. All you needed was to get some floatable object and a guaranteed line of supply. And thus it came to pass that all traffic on the high seas between 1981 and '83 appeared to be headed in one direction only—coracles, catamarans, freighters, dredgers, lighters, First World War ironclads, rafts from the Kon-Tiki expedition, converted oil barges, sailboats, and Mississippi paddleboats . . . anything at all that could limp into Lagos. The important thing was to arrive and be logged by the harbormaster, even if it meant anchoring fifty nautical miles away and going ashore in a lifeboat.

Now, please do not treat the following as part of the foregoing modest indulgence in poetic license, this is for real: The practice among some shipowners was to leave a junk ship laden with cement in Lagos harbor, fly its captain and crew back to Europe, sail another boat into Lagos harbor, and repeat the process. It cost those shipowners virtually nothing in comparison to the demurrage fees that the Nigerian government was obliged to pay for retaining those ships in the harbor while the foreigners kept crews in constant employment. All they had to do was leave a solitary crew member on board; they knew for a certainty that it would not be the turn of any boat for at least another three, possibly six months. Lagos harbors were such a sight that pilots on commercial airlines would deliberately fly over the flotilla—whose strings of lights transformed Lagos harbor into the most scintillating, extensive, and expensive Christmas tree in or out of season—and invite passengers not to miss the unique festival of light on the left or right side of the plane. The demurrage paid by the Nigerian government during this period was at least a hundred times the annual budget of several African nations put together.

A Coup against the Opposition

Now this was the spendthrift régime against which the military officers, led by Buhari, moved, a régime that created a permanent, infinitely expansive hole in budgetary declaration of intent with its infamous import license racket. That racket was one that permitted a party member, a friend or favored client of government, armed with such a document, to sit down in the courtyard of Ikoyi Hotel and make 1000 percent profit within an hour by selling his piece of paper to genuine manufacturers who had no other means of obtaining foreign exchange for their badly needed technical components. I personally witnessed one such creature sell a million-dollar license authorization for ten million in between his first glass of beer and the next. I had been alerted by a shocked American research student, a young woman in whom this party stalwart had taken more than a passing interest. His courtship method, as with others like him, was literally to oppress her with cash, assuring her that it came from virtually limitless sources. He was prepared to guarantee her a million dollars in pocket money during her stay, legally earned, if she would only succumb. And he proceeded to demonstrate how such money was made, quite openly, right in the courtyard of the bar in Ikoyi Hotel. I watched the transaction from my perch at the bar; it was quite commonplace.

You could say therefore that Buhari's military putsch had become inevitable, that it could actually set wrongs to right. The truth, however, is that Buhari and Idiagbon merely replaced one load of Nigerian rubbish with another, and of a far more sinister nature. In the economic sector, the substitution of what they described as "counter trade," a version of trade by barter, for the disreputable import license scheme simply left Nigeria's trading partners dictating the rate of exchange. It was also massively corruptible and was indeed put to corrupt exchanges. Even if, as I generally prefer to, we allow Buhari and Idiagbon the benefit of the doubt and accept that there is no proof that they did personally benefit from the avenues of corruption that were opened up by this system, there is no question whatever that their colleagues within the military and the usual business part-ners massively did.

When Babangida later took over power in August 1985 and detained the two leaders of that junta, he eventually set up a panel of civilian economists to investigate the operations of the so-called counter trade. This committee was headed by a friend of mine, the late Professor Aboyade, who visited and took evidence from the two detained leaders. The entire system, Aboyade told me, was a tightly sealed can within cans, within cans of worms. Fortunately, his experience in government, management, and economics provided him the can opener to reveal all that was hidden beneath the barrier of seals. The report has not been released till today, though the work of the committee was completed at least two years before Babangida was thrown out of office. Babangida's motives in inaugurating that inquiry, whose results, we do know, he never intended to make public, were, as always, complex and murky. Babangida was an assiduous gatherer of negative information about prospective threats; that much is easily established. It is likely, however, in my view, that Babangida was principally interested in seeing how others did it, to see if he could improve on their methods in the service of his already colossal personal wealth.

The question of probity or complicity of this duo in perpetuating corrupt practices carries the risk of becoming a bothersome distraction. Of far greater significance is the fundamental truth about these partners in terror: They wrote themselves into Nigerian, African, and possibly global history by staging a coup d'état, not against an incumbent government but against the opposition to that government. In short, Buhari and Idiagbon remain our most accomplished or at least most significant practitioners in the operations of the spoils of power.

True, Mr. Shehu Shagari, who was futilely engaged in running a government after the fraudulent elections, was indeed ejected from power. What is easy to forget is that the country had been made ungovernable by the frustrated rage of a cheated electorate. In response to that expanding state of public insurrection, on which actuality I had based my confident prediction in those already-mentioned articles in the foreign media, a number of radical young officers had also placed a coup in motion to oust the impostor and his gang of spendthrifts. Buhari struck first, however, and placed Shagari under a cozy house arrest in the posh residential area of Ikoyi, Lagos, while his well-tutored tribunal sentenced opposition leaders, in most cases, to several lifetimes in jail.

Anticipating the extra-legal intent of such a kangaroo tribunal, the Nigerian Bar Association had ordered a boycott of the proceedings by its members. Their stance was amply vindicated. Of the hundred cynical travesties of justice perpetrated by that tribunal, one need only recall the case of septuagenarian Pa Adekunle Ajasin, the erstwhile governor of Ondo state, held by the opposition party. He was arraigned three times on various charges of abuse of office, mismanagement of funds, and the like during his tenure, but even Buhari's obliging instrument could not in good conscience convict an obviously innocent man, indeed one whose tenure of office was marked by such probity, such frugal management of resources that his less inhibited colleagues had long consigned him to perdition. The common saying then was that it would take a Moses with his magic wand to make this rock of Ondo yield an unjustifiable or illegal trickle of moisture.

With every acquittal, Buhari's inquisitional team was sent back to work and prepared new charges, only to be confronted with the same dismissal of a patently hollow case. It was nothing personal. Buhari had resolved to run the country until the second coming of the Prophet, deputizing for that holy personage in the meantime. For this program, he needed to discredit the entire caste of politicians, but of course this was a selective discreditation agenda. Even while pronouncing all politicians bereft of vision and integrity, his actions were loaded against those who had consistently advertised such reprobates in their true colors, and these were largely the intellectuals and politicians both of the north and south, but especially the political opposition of the south and the middle belt. Of those who held office, the most revered was certainly Chief Michael Adekunle Ajasin.

Nothing therefore would satisfy this bilious duo until the old man was publicly tarred with the brush of corruption. Hence the tawdry drama of his court appearances, played in all cynicism before the bemused populace of Nigeria. It had an eerie echo of the trial of Christ himself at the hands of Pontius Pilate.

It went beyond the mission to expose, for public good, personal corruption or the corruption of a class, however. True, the self-vaunted moral crusaders dared not admit that they were persecuting at least one politician without blemish, but this particular personage, apart from being a state governor from the opposition party, also represented one of the historic pillars on which the Nigerian nation was built. Ajasin had to be destroyed, his symbolic stature reduced and his place in nation building erased. The nation was confronted, alas, with a dictatorship mentality that reached backwards in time to rewrite history. "*Après moi, le déluge*" was not sufficient for them. The text was augmented to read "*Et avant, le vide!*" Nothing before, nothing beyond, only the eternally extended present of a despotic imperative, trapped in delusions of immortality and anointed in the glow of spoils of power. Finally, Pa Ajasin was simply abandoned to a spell of indefinite detention in Agodi Prisons, Ibadan, convicted of no crime but that of his integrity.

It is instructive to contrast the tribulations of this elderly politician with the miraculous escape, after his arrest, of one of the most villainous of Shehu Shagari's aides, the secretary-general of the NPN, Alhaji Uba Ahmed, a northerner. Alhaji Ahmed arrived in Lagos on a UTA flight after the airport had been closed by the coup-makers. Planes were routinely diverted from

Ikeja, but the real reason was kept secret from the pilots. When the UTA pilot announced his plan to detour to Cotonou next door, Uba Ahmed marched into the cockpit and demanded that the pilot inform the control tower that he, VIP and all-powerful secretary-general of the ruling party, Uba Ahmed, was in the plane. Unless there was some overriding technical cause, an exception had to be made for his flight. The coup plotters' airport commandant could hardly believe his luck! He must have rubbed his hands in glee at this unexpected booty, oblivious of the *real* nature of the coup, ignorant of the autonomous laws that govern the spoils of power. Coups, after all, thought the ignorant man, are made against incumbent governments, and so, on that rational assumption, he welcomed the opportunity of seizing the secretary-general of the discredited party. Probably he was already basking in the commendations he would receive for quick thinking.

So he gave special permission for this landing, requesting that the pilot convey his apologies to the nearly inconvenienced voyager and ordered the plane to taxi to the VIP parking lot. As the plane landed, Uba Ahmed encountered what he first thought was a guard of honor. His chagrin may be imagined when he found that he was under arrest. He was whisked off to detention in Bonny Barracks.

After which, the lies began. I recall Buhari's face when he was questioned by the press on television about the miraculous disappearance of Uba Ahmed a day or two after he was locked up in Bonny Camp. His face broke into a self-conscious, sheepish grin as he tried to contradict established facts, including his own government's affirmation of Uba Ahmed's arrest. We need only add, as a footnote, that Uba Ahmed, after escaping from custody and fleeing the country, returned to his home in the north several times during Buhari's régime, flying in boldly through the international airport in Kano. Buhari's régime vaunted itself as the most thorough, ruthless, and disciplined that Nigeria would ever experience, yet, one after the other, the most criminally liable of Shagari's officers—both within party and government—left the country, came in and out as they pleased, while Buhari's tribunal sentenced opposition figures to spells of between a hundred and three hundred years in prison for every dubious kind of crime. The upshot of the "rigidity" and corrective zeal of that reign of terror was indisputable: a partisan scale of judgment, weighed heavily against progressives, especially all those, from whatever part of the country, who were considered a serious threat to the hegemonic design of a self-perpetuating clique from the yet feudally oriented part of the country, whose leaders remain backward in their thinking, reactionary and nepotistic in political orientation, a clique that is still made up largely of unproductive scions of a moribund social order that has earned itself such titles—not always accurate but always instructive—as the Kaduna or Northern Mafia, feudal irredentists, Dan Fodio Jihadists, and the Sokoto Caliphate. It is this group whose protective umbrella is hoisted over loyal slaves like Inspector General of Police Adewusi and guarantees them perpetual immunity.

This minority, let it be understood, is profoundly insecure. It lords its existence directly over a restless, increasingly articulate and politically aware mass of northerners who are no longer satisfied with the pittance that comes to them in a carefully nurtured tradition of condescension and patronage. Among its elite, there have been several instances of organized and militant resistance, of whom notable intellectuals like Bala Usman, the late Bala Mohammed, and politicians such as Balarabe Musa, the late Aminu Kano, and even military officers like Colonel Umar have become outspoken challengers of this doomed but disruptive status quo, the jealous guardians of the spoils of power. Bala Mohammed, it must be mentioned, died a particularly gruesome death, hacked and burnt in his own house by a mob that was incited by the threatened feudal order, and with the full coopera-tion of the police, the props of Shehu Shagari's doomed régime. The police chief in charge of order—or disorder—on that day, just for historic interest, countered accusations of collaboration in this daylight murder by entering the expression "cooperative mob" in the Nigerian dictionary of mayhem. There was nothing he could have done to arrest the situation because, he said, his men had only witnessed the activities of a "cooperative mob."

The "War against Indis'plin"

That was the slogan, but never was a war seen to be waged with such consistent virulence against the disciplined and progres-sive. Not even the most implacable enemy of the late Chief Obafemi Awolowo, leader of the opposition Unity Party of Nigeria, would deny that here was one man in all of the Nigerian population for whom the word "disciplined" was originally coined. Yet Obafemi Awolowo's Ikenne home became the junta's first port of call once the coup had succeeded, and a violent incursion it manifestly was.

They came at dawn and turned his home inside out. Remarka-bly, the home of President Shehu Shagari was not subjected to any such raid. Equally exempted were the homes of his principal lieutenants—ministers, party leaders, and so on—who obviously bore responsibility for the conditions that could be held to justify military intervention. Such few raids as were undertaken took place weeks and months later, long after any sensible horse would have bolted from the stable, and were conducted by an apologetic, collaborative police, not by the species of military storm troopers who flooded Awolowo's Ikenne home and placed

it under a dawn siege almost simultaneously with the announcement of the coup.

In the end, the military would claim that certain "restricted"
documents had been found in his library and proceed to ejacu-
late menacing growls that portended his likely arrest and per-
secution. What, however, was the truth about those documents?
They did indeed contain sensitive material, sent anonymously to
the chief by his mostly volunteer intelligence network within
the army and even the secret services. One particular document
had to do with the complicity of some highly placed military
figures in defrauding the nation of close to $2.8 billion from the
oil revenue.

Buhari and Company were in a rage. Lieutenant Colonel
Mamman Vatsa, a versifier of social musings, later to be executed
for his alleged role in the attempted coup against General
Babangida's régime, told a number of writers, myself included,
that Awolowo would be put on trial. However, as we say in our
part of the world, even the insensate child distinguishes between
the keen edge of the knife and the flat. Buhari and Company
contented themselves with confiscating Awolowo's passport and
mounting a suffocating surveillance on his home. It was the
earliest indication, as the media and other public commentators
wryly observed, that Buhari's intervention was no coup but a
negotiated change of attire by Shagari and his party, the NPN.

The travails of the human rights campaigner Dr. Tai Solarin,
another icon of public discipline, was not unconnected with the
raid on Chief Awolowo's home and the seizure of "restricted"
documents. Tai had been a consistent and unrepentant thorn in
the hide of the overthrown president Shehu Shagari, and he
wasted no time in demanding from the new interlopers a definite
date for their return to barracks. The latter act provided the
public excuse needed by Buhari to stomp on the gadfly, but let us
keep in mind that Buhari constantly sought and exacted revenge

on all those whom, in that perverse pattern of reasoning we have outlined, he held responsible for exposing Shagari as the failure he was. There was a more immediate grudge, however. Tai Solarin, a close supporter and confidant of Chief Obafemi Awolowo, though not a party card carrier at the time, was suspected to have shared some knowledge of the missing $2.8 billion with the chief, since he often made public statements on the affair. Many Nigerians could not understand why, when a phony commission of inquiry was emplaced by Shagari to look into this missing sum, Tai Solarin would not reveal the source of information for his public accusations. By contrast, another sleuth on the track of the missing billions, the brilliant engineering professor Awojobi, came to the tribunal with masses of files filled with calculations as well as documents somehow extracted from the ministry. Tai Solarin, to the disappointment of his admirers, put up a publicly embarrassing performance. He would only insist that he heard of the missing sum on a public bus, a ridiculous and irresponsible basis for accusations to emanate from such a respected voice, if that was indeed the case. The truth, however, was that Tai could not disclose what he knew and how he knew it. Apart from an obligation not to disclose his source—Tai was also a practicing journalist—some crucial documentation was now beyond his reach, having been carted away in that initial raid on Awolowo's house.

The venom with which Buhari mistreated Tai Solarin indicated quite clearly that Tai was paying a penalty that was totally disproportionate to his "crime" of calling for a definitive date for the termination of this new dictatorship. Buhari was minister of petroleum under General Olusegun Obasanjo when the magic sum had allegedly staged its disappearing act, and thus the plot, as they say, veritably thickened.

Now it was that same Buhari who displaced Shagari and became the new head of state. Buhari was a man of speed. He left the nation dizzy by the tempo he adopted, leaping from nation-muzzling decrees to sanitation exercises, introducing record-breaking prison sentences of two and three hundred years, then springing to decongest the ports with bravura. He was the man who publicly said, "Yes, I intend to tamper with the press," and promptly introduced the infamous Decree No. 2, which declared any journalist guilty, with a penalty of prison without option of fine, not for publishing lies against the government or its officials but for publishing the truth, if such truths brought the government or any of its officials into public ridicule and contempt. The guilty publishing house would also be sentenced to pay a fine. Buhari and his clone, Idiagbon, were instant miracle workers, breaking the sound barrier, since they tended to arrive at the next action spot even before the pronouncement was dry on the airwaves.

The nation therefore deserved to be forgiven for permitting itself to be thrilled and on tenterhooks with expectation when, barely giving himself time to become accustomed to his new exalted position, Buhari invaded his old ministry, seized all the files, swearing that he was resolved to get to the bottom of all allegations regarding the vanished billions and inform the Nigerian people accordingly. A whole year passed in silence. The next began, and that was the last the Nigerian populace would hear, till today, of the $2.8 billion affair.

Dr. Awojobi was dead (he died of hypertension, some say, precipitated by his obsession with this affair); some officers whose names had cropped up repeatedly during the public rounds of speculations and revelations were redeployed, some who had been retired under Shagari were brought back; but the sum total of this energetic investigation, handled personally by the dis'plin despot, was silence! And that was also the fate of Tai Solarin, an asthmatic patient, banished to Maiduguri prisons, where the climate was especially harmful to him, given his ailment. There, he virtually battled for his life until he was transferred to the somewhat more congenial climate of Kaduna prisons. He was to remain there, like other victims of Buhari, until the fall of that moral crusader, to whom, as I have stated, I join others in extending the cloak of innocence until absolutely proved guilty.

A Prophet without Honor

Buhari was a remorseless collector of captives. He took delight in raiding the camp of the opposition to the previous régime while curiously leaving the camp of the man he had displaced, Shehu Shagari, virtually untouched. The exceptions were either members of the internal opposition within Shagari's camp—such as Audu Ogbe, the minister of communications—or else nonentities within the ranks who were served up as sacrificial lambs to assuage the suspicions of the public. Among Buhari's crop, the case of Ebenezer Babatope remains especially intriguing, even till today, perhaps as a pointer to Buhari's psychological conditioning. Accused at no time of any crime, never brought to trial even as a witness, Babatope was simply locked away in prison in the far north. On the death of his father while in prison, no pleas from any direction made the slightest dent in Buhari's shield against humaneness; Batatope was not permitted to attend, even under escort, his father's funeral.

On the surface, the case of Ebenezer Babatope falls into the general pattern of the elimination of opposition voices. Babatope had been a director of research and campaigner for Chief Obafemi Awolowo's Unity Party of Nigeria. He had in fact planned to take a sabbatical from politics once the elections were over and travel to England to read for a higher law degree, which was exactly what he did. At no time had he participated in government, not even in those states where the UPN had won elections. Babatope was, quite simply, a paid employee of the party bureaucracy. He had committed an unlisted crime, however, of which he remained blissfully unaware. And so, he blithely proceeded to England, filed his admission papers, and secured an apartment when Buhari struck. With equal insouciance, he returned home to attend to unfinished family business, intending to go back to Buckingham University shortly to commence his studies.

However, about a year before the contentious 1983 elections, in a published article, Babatope had warned of General Buhari's political ambitions, urging lovers of democracy to watch out for the gangling officer; he cited as evidence an address that Buhari had made at a military passing-out parade. When Buhari did, finally, fulfill Babatope's prediction, he must have gnashed his teeth in frustration on discovering that the bird had flown. He needed not have worried. Babatope, like Uba Ahmed, obliged him by returning home, but there the similarities ended. Buhari promptly ordered his men to make a beeline for the home of the prophet and lock him up in Gashua, a remote prison in the far north of Nigeria. According to the delegation that went to intercede on behalf of the hapless man, the still-incensed dictator barely entertained the spelling out of their mission. He informed them brusquely that he had ordered his men to throw the key of the cell into the bush because "that Babatope will remain in prison until he rots." Indeed, a prophet hath honour. . . .

The Exception and the Rule: The Crated Minister

The notion that there are two distinct sets of laws operating within the nation has become increasingly difficult to dismiss, and the tragedy for the nation lies in the fact that it is the army, a supposedly unified body, whose interventions provide the greatest evidence for this and aggravate the tensions caused by an unequal application of power. The politics of revenge reached its climax during the rule of Buhari and Idiagbon, and this was all the more devastating because this was a junta whose "color-blind" rhetoric proved to be a camouflage for a lack of moral vision.

Of course there were exceptions that appear to belie the pattern. Objectors would be quick to point out the fact that it was Buhari who, after all, had attempted to repatriate Shagari's principal jobman and fellow northerner, Umaru Dikko, in a wooden crate right under the nose of that redoubtable defender of democratic values, Dame Margaret Thatcher, a botched operation that involved an officer from the Nigerian army, Israeli mercenaries, and an attaché at the Nigerian mission in London.

Umaru Dikko was the uncrowned prime minister to Shehu Shagari's presidency. Together with Uba Ahmed, the secretary-general, and perhaps Chief Adisa Akinloye, chairman of the party, he made up the triumvirate that can be rightly credited with running Shehu Shagari's presidency from within the party. He was the overall boss of the infamous Presidential Task Force on Rice Importation, which joined hands with the cement armada and the import license racket to deplete the Nigerian treasury to an extent that has yet to be accurately assessed, but from which the nation has yet to recover. Umaru earned even greater infamy by dismissing all warnings about wastage of resources, the collapsing economy, and domestic hardship in the words "Nigerians have not yet begun to eat from the dustbins."

Was Buhari taking up cudgels on behalf of the Nigerian masses whose privations were dismissed in such a cavalier manner by one of the principal architects of that social and economic collapse? Nigerians applauded the attempt to crate back Umaru

Dikko to his native land, but what were Buhari's real motivations? On whose behalf was the inept bandit raid conducted?

The answer to that is twofold. First, Umaru Dikko had gone
even further than Babatope. His was not simply a matter of
deductive prophesying; he had prior knowledge of Buhari's coup
and had warned Shehu Shagari about the plot. He even provided
a list of the names of the principals, in his own handwriting, a list
that was found on Shagari's desk by Buhari's men when they took
over the president's office. Next, and this was even more serious,
Umaru Dikko had broken rank. After his miraculous "escape,"
another episode of significance, from the general rounding-up of
Shagari's collaborators, he established himself in London as a
voice of opposition, set up a newspaper, and generally consti-
tuted himself into a veritable threat against the survival of Buhari.
Unlike Uba Ahmed, the other notable escapee from his privileged part of the country, Umaru Dikko simply would not lie low
and shut up! He had disqualified himself from benefiting from
the spoils of power; he had to be dealt with as a lesson to others.

In any case, has Umaru Dikko, once a trapped rat in a wooden
cage, not since returned to his beloved Nigeria, this time in a
presidential plane, on special invitation by the incumbent head
of state, with a red carpet reception and all trimmings? He
returned in triumph to where he had departed as a hunted
fugitive and promptly announced that he was back to rescue
Nigeria from itself and deal thoroughly with all his detractors.
Umaru Dikko's plane rolled into Abuja almost at the very
moment that the rightful head of state, President-elect Moshood
Abiola, was being driven round the various prisons of northern
Nigeria, in a Black Maria (or meat-wagon elsewhere) for the
heinous crime of winning a free and fair election and the even
more treasonable offense of insisting on his electoral mandate.

With an injured spine, Abiola was given the ride of his life,
Steve Biko style, perhaps in the hope that such an unaccustomed

ride would break the will of the millionaire by giving him a foretaste of what was yet to come. It could be of course this was not the original intent; certainly Abacha's security police were discomfited by the fact that, no matter how remote a prison was found in what they presumed was a hostile north, the populace began a spontaneous pilgrimage to his place of detention. At times, word of his arrival preceded him and the police vehicles were met by enthusiastic crowds. So again and again came the instructions "Move him on, find somewhere else," until after a vicious odyssey of some four thousand kilometers (about twenty-five hundred miles), Abiola was brought back to starting point, Abuja, where Sani Abacha felt he could at least anticipate the action of his supporters.

Where It All Began

The spoils of power spell protection, immunity; unlike the spoils of office, the former remain guaranteed long after office. Often the system is based on the dynastic imperative, be this by recognized identity or deriving from actuality. Babangida's physical disposition at this moment, in a luxurious, fortified mansion that is guarded by hordes of soldiers who owe him absolute loyalty, indicates that he remains part of that charmed circle of the penumbra of spoils. In a different sense, certainly from a tacit bipartisan conspiracy that is so uniquely American, you could say that Richard Nixon continued to enjoy the spoils of power even after being disgraced from office. Instead of being carted off to Sing Sing, he obtained a presidential pardon. His rehabilitation attained heights that turned him into America's high-profile ambassador, earned him a state funeral, and recently, apotheosization on a postage stamp.

How Hastings Banda of Malawi must envy him, or his fellow criminal from the other end of the ideological axis—Mariam Mengistu, the mass murderer of Ethiopia. How they must envy even Shehu Shagari, whose aftermath still provides us the longest running instance of the smooth mechanisms of the spoils of power in that western region of the African continent; it simply runs on and on even till today and remains at the crisis of the Nigerian will to identity.

The phenomenon at the heart of this discourse is mostly peculiar to Nigeria. Ghana and Mali appear to be free from it, as witness the punishment meted out to the ousted dictator in Mali and the unprecedented bloody crop of three ex-generals at a blow, publicly executed after the second coming of Jerry Rawlings in Ghana. Nowhere in these and most other West African countries are the spoils of power thus routinely handed down from villain to villain and extended retroactively to shield past villains. By contrast, in our own case, the overriding lesson as a restricted list of scions are groomed in the tradition is this: Privilege must never be abandoned nor conceded to others outside the hegemonic circle. The members meet and choose a flag bearer. His only concession to the rest of the nation is that he learns when to permit a trickle of the spoils of office, but not of power, to fall through his fingers where necessary, to douse the smouldering resentment of others—the enlightened, the rejected, or the merely ambitious. This is why the nation called Nigeria will never realize her true self until the guardians stop treating power as a repository of spoils, regarding it instead as a responsibility whose weight must be evenly distributed for a national equilibrium.

Three observations from a depressing catalogue need to be extracted and stressed: First, the north is not a monolithic bastion of reaction, that north itself being contested by progressives who indeed sometimes bear, as has been seen, the most horrible consequences for "betraying their class." Second, the reactionary clique is just as determined to preserve the status quo and, in its strategies of self-consolidation, marks down what it perceives as political sophistication, such as egalitarian credos or faith in meritocracy (certainly most notable in the south) as its greatest threat. And finally, the subornation—and when that fails, humiliation—of southern leadership thus becomes a cornerstone in the overall strategy toward the last stated goal. The purpose of this is clear: to make those southern troublemakers lose confidence in their leadership and thus render them divided, cynical, and vulnerable. This has created a marked trend in the conduct of power that I have termed the politics of revenge. And to buttress the foregoing and bring the cycle to an ironic close, we must now narrate the background of the presently embattled president-elect of Nigeria, Moshood M. K. O. Abiola.

We are back in 1979, the attempt at a second republic after two decades of military rule—Aguiyi-Ironsi, Yakubu Gowon, Murtala Mohammed, Olusegun Obasanjo (all generals before or after). The last, General Obasanjo, has turned the politicians loose, and political parties are now in the process of formation. Moshood Abiola, a southerner, becomes one of the founding members of that same political party, the NPN of Shehu Shagari. With his usual energy and total commitment, he throws himself into the creation of the party, funding it generously and nurturing it with the very undemocratic methods that we have already observed in the tendencies of that party.

The NPN, let it be conceded, did attract some genuine nationalists who were convinced that its declarations indicated a true attempt to create a national party; this is not the place to suggest that it was this touted virtue that attracted Moshood Abiola to the party. It is more likely that he realized that his own presidential ambitions would be more easily achieved within that party rather than in the other major party, the Unity Party of Nigeria, which was headed by Chief Obafemi Awolowo, a veteran whose leadership was bound to be unchallengeable as long as he was alive.

In terms of hierarchical mobility at least, the NPN was, on the surface, a more democratic organization. The top post was open to competition whereas, in the UPN, only a maverick out for some political fun and self-publicizing rascality would think of contending the top position with Awolowo. Again, this requires some qualification, as those who were close to Awolowo and knew him well insist that the Grand Old Man would have welcomed any such fight, confident in his ability to pulverize his opponent.

The NPN also had the plausible "unifying" system by which it was stipulated that the major positions would go round the country, which was thereby zoned for that very purpose. For instance, if the chairmanship of the party came from the south, candidacy for the presidential position would go to the north. And both positions would be rotated after each successful election. All this was entered into the party constitution and bruited nationwide to promote the nation-unifying credentials of that party. The NPN rode successfully on the crest of this power-sharing principle, which would usher in a new era of detribalized politics. Even the outgoing military dictator, General Olusegun Obasanjo, a southerner and a Yoruba, never missed an opportunity to contrast the NPN advantageously with its rival, the UPN, decrying the latter as a one-man Yoruba tribalistic southern party. Obasanjo's real motives for his support of the NPN and his blatant manipulation of Shagari into power as his successor were of course far more complex, as many did insist at the time and as events have certainly proved. Obasanjo had a curious romance with the northern hegemony, perhaps it was more a fear; this is a subject that must be taken up in another place, taking account of observations of many who were close to him and who have been sufficiently intrigued to discuss this trait of insecurity in a military head of state. Let us simply state here that he later rued his inclinations and his action and acknowledges today that he was only another naive tool in the deep scheming of that northern clique. He was last heard of attempting to forge a southern front against the notorious "mafia" and has even taken to attending the meetings of Egbe Afenifere, a purely ethnic organization dedicated, openly and unapologetically, to the promotion of Yoruba political interests.*

In 1979, the chairmanship of the NPN had gone to a Yoruba, that is, a southerner, while the presidency was assigned to the north. The NPN, with a little help from the outgoing régime of Obasanjo, won that election. There is little doubt, in my view, that the NPN obtained the largest number of votes of all the five contending parties. The electoral laws were clear, however, about the next stage if any one party failed to emerge overall winner, a common-enough provision in a number of democracies. The definition of this, inscribed in electoral law, was that such a party must, in addition to winning the highest total number of votes, take at least one-third of the votes in two-thirds of the states. The word "state" is as employed in that electoral decree. That provision provided the nation with its first democratic hurdle as the results began to come in.

Now what is two-thirds of any number whose units happen to be indivisible by three? To begin with, what is one-third of seven chairs? Standard, time-tested arithmetic decrees very clearly that

---

*Alas, since this was written, Obasanjo has himself fallen victim of the "politics of revenge." Arrested for alleged complicity in a mysterious coup plot against Sani Abacha, he was recently tried in secret and sentenced to twenty-five years in prison. The secret tribunal continues, with new charges. From the latest report, there will be trials "in absentia."

this means two and one-third, which in turn means two. There is no such thing as half a chair; it ceases to be a chair when it is halved or thirded (no such word, I know). Two-thirds of seven chairs equally mean four and two-thirds, only this time the fraction is unified upwards to read five. I merely reiterate common arithmetical usage. However, Nigerians, and the press especially, were determined to leave nothing to chance.

Ovie-Whiskey, a retired judge and chairman of the electoral commission, was brought to the radio and television studios to clarify the weighty mathematical problem. The nation is made up of nineteen states, he was reminded. What exactly, then, is the answer to the question about two-thirds of nineteen states? Before the entire Nigerian nation as witness, Ovie-Whiskey declared again and again that two-thirds of nineteen in this context is thirteen. Both he and his staff clarified this further: What the electoral law means by the two-thirds requirement is that, to win in the first round, a candidate, in addition to scoring the highest total number of votes, must also have won at least one-third of the votes in *each* of thirteen states. This statement of the chairman of the electoral commission was carried in all Nigerian newspapers. It was consistently drummed into public consciousness whenever the question came up, by the commission's secretaries, public enlightenment officers, and others. Nigerians prepared to troop out to vote on that clear understanding while the parties mapped out their strategies, hopefully for winning on the first ballot by fulfilling those conditions and, failing that, for later alliances at the electoral college if no one party succeeded in a first-round victory. Those conditions were, need one add, justified by the military régime as a way to ensure that any winner must have a reasonable amount of support outside his or her own state in a spread that was bound to foster national unity.

When the results began to emerge, however, and it became clear that Shehu Shagari's party had failed to attain the required one-third votes in two-thirds of the states, a party lawyer, Richard Akinjide, was produced suddenly on television to propose a novel interpretation of that electoral law. One-third of the total votes from two-thirds of the states did mean, he declared, one-third of the votes cast in twelve and two-thirds of the states, not thirteen. This would then mean in turn one-third of the votes cast in twelve of the states, plus one-third of two-thirds of the votes cast in one more state.

If you are confused, be assured that I am even more so. Just take it from me that it all amounts to this: The goalposts were shifted after the goal was missed, and the referee then awarded a goal because the ball went where the goalposts should have been. But I am fairly certain that I have given a true version of the mathematical innovation unveiled to the nation *after* the voting, *after* the announcement of results had begun. Whether lawyer Richard Akinjide does prove in the end to be the Albert Einstein of Nigeria still appears to me totally beside the question. The government of General Olusegun Obasanjo signaled its complicity by immediately approving the setup proposition; it had, in any case, begun the handing-over process to Shehu Shagari, even to the extent of consulting him about, then appointing his choice of, Chief Justice to fill the vacant position in the Supreme Court.

The courts were waiting for the aggrieved parties; they rejected their petition and upheld the modern mathematics of the Nigerian Einstein.

The Supreme Court, the final arbiter, proceeded to make legal history. It upheld the decision of the lower courts (with one dissenting voice) but it also entered a historic caveat hitherto unheard-of in Nigerian judicial annals. Those learned judges added, without a quiver of embarrassment, that their judgement could not be cited in future as a precedent!

In the dust thrown up by this open violation of the stated electoral arithmetic, no one appeared to have noticed that there was one state, Gongola, whose results had not yet been announced. The NPN had not even won one-third in the twelfth state, had not even won in that state at all. The results were deliberately withheld until the scores of the NPN and UPN could be switched. It was done through radio transmission from that far-flung state. And this was effected with the connivance of the outgoing military régime who lived in mortal fear, just as the British colonial powers had lived, of a political figure such as Obafemi Awolowo emerging as leader of a potentially powerful African nation. The irony of the Nigerian crisis today is that the imprisoned president-elect, M. K. O. Abiola, was himself not an innocent in this affair. This, then, is the true story of how Shehu Shagari became president of the Republic of Nigeria in the first democratic elections after a long military spell. That was 1979.

Came 1983 and the next round of elections. We have already been submerged in the state brutality and physical violence that accompanied those elections and been schooled in the violence done to mathematics in the earlier '79 elections. It is time to touch on a different quality of violence—the psychological, a fitting intraparty prelude to the physical that would mark the actual campaigns among the parties in 1983. Without question, the brutality of the Shagari-run police during those elections is directly traceable to that act of psychological bruising that eroded the NPN support in the south and left the incumbent power only one course of action—massive repression.

At the party convention, the NPN south duly staked its claim, with M. K. O. Abiola as its contender. The party convention of that year, however, was to prove for the millionaire a political landmark in perfidy. Without warning, on the very floor of that convention, the party rules were rewritten. Abiola's northern allies, led by the erstwhile nationalists such as Adamu Ciroma, Uba Ahmed, Umaru Dikko, and Ibrahim Tahir, told Abiola to his face that the 1979 agreement was a one-time arrangement only and that the candidacy was now open to all comers.

While Abiola was waiting out his turn during Shagari's tenure, the northern cabal had consolidated its hold on the party, perfected its strategies for holding on to power in secret caucuses. Moshood Abiola, by contrast, had simply performed his duties—indeed, over and above the call—as a party faithful, making no effort whatever to mobilize any numerical support within the party. The candidacy, he and his fellow southerners had understood, was his for the taking, bar the usual convention formalities.

Not so, said Umaru Dikko, who provided the unkindest cut of all. In a callous dismissal of Abiola's notorious generosity to party coffers, a generosity that was certainly remarkable even by that party's ostentatious culture of social insensitivity, Umaru Dikko declared that the presidential candidacy was not "for sale to the highest bidder." Even those northern party insiders whom Abiola had regarded as personal, intimate friends, not merely political colleagues, virtually rebuked him for his overweening ambition.

Abiola himself narrated to me an encounter between him and Shagari after the latter had announced his intention to stand for a second term of office. They met in Shagari's presidential office at the incumbent's own request. He wanted to "talk things over," to see if a way could be found to soothe his rival and keep the party from foundering over the "minor misunderstanding." Shagari appeared anxious not to lose southern support, in view of the coming elections. So Abiola asked him what had become of what he had regarded as a cast-iron arrangement to shift the presidency to the south after the first term. Replied Shagari, "Well, Chief, you know, it is all in the natural order of things. A country is just like a farm where everyone has his functions. Allah has willed it that someone must hold the cow by the horns while another does the milking."* He then asked Abiola what compensation he would accept from him as president. Oil lifting perhaps? How many barrels a day would satisfy him?

According to Abiola, he told Shagari that all he wanted from him was the seat he then occupied, nothing more or less. By rights, he, Abiola, should be the one to offer Shagari petroleum allocation as his retirement benefits after serving the nation so loyally for the agreed-upon tenure of office. And then, his choler rising, he began to tell Shagari exactly what he felt about the analogy of the cow and horns and milk. . . . The meeting, needless to say, ended on that note. Shortly after, he resigned from the party. Abiola did admit to me, however, that he eventually sent Shagari a list of party faithfuls whom he felt deserved their own share of the oil bonanza; that list consisted of names of his supporters within the party whose loyalty, he decided, should be rewarded.

Abiola, it would appear, was destined to be the catalyst for the ultimate revelation of the feudalist fixation of those whom, by contrast, their intellectual and political peers in other parts of the nation had accepted, on their part, as equal partners in a national enterprise. Publicly humiliated, he announced his resignation from the party and his withdrawal from politics altogether. From then on, he would devote himself to his business and to philanthropic acts that cut a wide, unprecedented swath across the country, across religion and ethnic considerations. He donated without bias to religious-leaning organizations, building mosques and Islamic institutions with as much zeal as he donated to churches and Christian enterprises.

The triumph of his treacherous colleagues in that 1983 election was to be short-lived, however, as, a few months into the renewed mandate of Shehu Shagari, the military struck, and Buhari and Idiagbon unleashed their own brand of terrorism on

*See Appendix I.

the nation. Buhari moved resolutely to humiliate and emasculate southern political leadership while he consolidated himself in power. The flag bearers of the hegemonic tendency had proved incompetent, and so he assumed that mandate indefinitely, banned all discussion of a return to civilian rule. The rhetoric of a neutral instrument of correction was effective and credible only for a limited time; thereafter, scepticism and suspicion took over. The jubilations at his overthrow were some of the most ebullient in the history of Nigerian coups.

A decade later, almost to the date, a new chapter was opened in the tract of the politics of vengeance, only this time the very nadir of intelligence has been breached and a creature of pure instinct, a sheer carapace of brutality and superstition, has been dredged up from the slurry to take control of the lives of Nigerians. Surrounded by the most incorrigible of a dwindling tribe of northern hegemonists, he is kept impervious to the subtleties of power and the seduction of a positive historic mention. He is a creature of proven rapacity who has not only consumed a lion's share of the nation's resources but has begun to consume his erstwhile collaborators and, next, his own nest. Too late, even his mentors in the politics of vengeance will realize that their underling is incapable of recognizing the delimitations of the political geography of revenge. They will wake up in astonishment to find that they now constitute the objects of revenge: In his eyes they will read the fatal accusation: "You kept me too long from my hidden destiny!"

Postscript

It fell to Maitama Sule, a much-revered, astute scion of the northern oligarchy with a distinguished stint as Nigerian ambassador to the United Nations, to make the definitive annunciation of the gospel of this northern elite. Until his public statement, the response of this northern minority to charges of conspiracy for feudal absolutism had been mostly dismissive jeers, solemn denials, deliberate evasions, and confusion of the issue through recourse to "statistical proofs," such as publication of lists of highly placed southerners in civil service positions, banking directorships, and chairmanships of boards. Driven eventually to abandon a childish denial or obfuscation of the obvious, their intellectuals then developed the theory of power equalization. Simply put, they argued to their own satisfaction that the southern part of the country had a control of economic power; therefore, it was only just that the north should hang on to political power.

Maitama Sule put an end to all such casuistry. An elegant speaker whose greatest asset is a disarming guilelessness, he cast aside all further tergiversation and, like Shehu Shagari, simply made himself a humble spokesman of the Divine Will. God, he declared, had wisely shared different talents among us Nigerians. The easterners, the Igbos, for instance, are the business entrepreneurs. The west, the Yoruba, make excellent administrators, civil servants, and teachers. The north, the Hausas, are blessed with the gift of leadership and must be accepted as such.

The responsibility for undoing the damage done to the national sense of belonging and both individual and collective sensibilities rests on the shoulders of our own peers in the north—the Balarabe Musa, Bala Usman, and the younger generation represented by the Ahmadu Abubakar, Colonel Umar, and so on. They do not have an enviable task, but it is they who must wrest effective leadership from this endless travesty that continues to unmask even the least-suspected role models of the north, such as Alhaji Maitama Sule!

The National Question:
Internal Imperatives

*L*et us recapitulate, but placing emphasis this time on the interior mechanics of the nation space, especially as it provides for or deprives the inmates of the means to life, self-worth, and productive existence.

Every thinking inhabitant of a given national space must surely, at some moment or the other of his existence, reflect upon the significance, or none, of his or her own identity as it relates to the existing or historical definitions of that space. This questioning may have a simple focus, such as language, one that is taken no further once it is, to all appearances, satisfactorily resolved—the Welsh, for instance, or the Occitans in France, the Berbers in Algeria, or indeed the Hispanics in the United States. It could also be manifested in a wider cultural awareness, a restless sense of identity that dangerously stresses the casing of a common nationality. Economic arrangements may also provide the causative factor, usually the unsatisfactory aspects as they are perceived by different groupings within the overall national body. This last factor—expressed in the language of "unequal development," "unfair revenue allocation," "regional neglect," et cetera—is invariably a triggering mechanism for the recollection of some other identity, independent of the foregoing or related, one that has been subsumed, never mind how briefly or how historically dated, beneath existing assumptions or impositions of nation being. The Soviet Union provides the most chastening instance of this.

Less known, for now, is the tragic example of the Ogoni people, victims of a genocidal onslaught by a singularly vicious military dictatorship in my own Nigeria. The Ogoni predicament has provoked, sometimes in the most unexpected quarters, this exercise in national introspection. By this I refer to open debates that increasingly posit the assumptions of nation being— be it as an ideal, a notional bonding, a provider, a haven of security and order, or an enterprise of productive coexistence— against the direct experience of the actual human composition within the nation. This is when we are confronted with the ground rule that any nation apprehension that takes its being in ideas outside the humanity that is the fundamental element of its very existence is as vaporous as the nation itself. (Ask yourselves, why do the citizens of the United States of America periodically set upon their flag, trample on it and burn it? What makes the phenomenon so prevalent as to require legislation that criminalizes this act of rejection and desecration? Why is there today an extremist tendency that has even resulted in the formation of local militia, one that accuses the state of becoming a structure of alienation and involves taking up arms to defend novel states of nation definition?)

Sadly, this ground rule is not as universal as it deserves to be, or at best, it is one that rarely transcends lip service. The truth is, some conceive of a nation almost in terms of gross national product, others—a diminishing, almost vanished breed entirely—see nation being as a material manifestation of a remorseless, historical process that they of course are singularly privileged to preconceive and direct. And yet others, with increasing virulence in recent times, conceive the nation as an expression of divine will whose active processes, from private conduct to the arts, from fiscal policies to architectural designs, must be governed by the desire to win approbation of and/or reflect and glorify the omnipotence and grandeur of the Invisible Presence. To many, the "City of God" is not a metaphor, unless it is a mere diminutive for the "Nation of God." Even as I speak, perhaps the fiftieth journalist is being murdered in Algeria in the name of a supreme deity and his apotheosized prophet. The figure last stood at forty-seven, but that was all of a week or two ago.

If only the sacrifices demanded of the human polity for the actualization of such extraterrestrial perceptions of society were limited to a failure to consult that humanity, even by proxy! If only the affected had nothing worse to complain of than the failure of such a divinely endowed elite to make the rest an active part, not a coerced, cowed, and submissive pawn in what, after all, are undertakings within and on behalf of the total community, one might be able to shrug off the questionable priorities that result from such arrogation of power and resources by a few on behalf of the entirety! Alas, the consequences are often more than a mere emotive response that comes from the sense of being ignored. However, let us not burden our emotions with the statistics of sneak murders that are being planned or executed, at this moment, in a country like Egypt or Algeria, all in the name of the divine will. We shall attempt the easier task and restrict ourselves to the theme of development and the politics of development, asking whether or not we can identify any stronger criteria for addressing a populated space as a nation.

Let us take a distressed environment, impoverished, slum-ridden. Disobeying all laws of organic development, it is made to undergo the intrusion of a dominating, environmentally disproportionate structure; well, even this could be endured. If the existence of such a structure had no deleterious social consequences, right from conception to realization, one could console oneself with the resultant monumental landmarks, some of them of frankly enduring and aesthetic properties. But we do know that these heaven-directed labors of love are achieved at the expense of the fundamental well-being of the human entities below.

The replication of Saint Peter's Basilica in remote Yamoussoukro, birthplace of the late Ivorian president, or the no less extravagant "triumph of modern architectural engineering," that being one of the more restrained descriptions of the mosque in Casablanca: Are these really expressions of devotion to the unseen or delusions of grandeur, the craving for self-immortalization by some individuals who happened to find or to manipulate themselves into positions where, without the responsibility for statutory accounting, the entire treasury of a nation is placed at their personal disposal? The question is whether private whims, even of the deepest religious coloring, are really a rational substitute for the systematic identification of development priorities for a nation. All we can be certain of (because it is clearly provable) is that the proliferation of grandiose cathedrals, basilicas, temples, mosques, shrines, and other places of worship throughout the global landscape has not perceptibly improved the living conditions or moral sensibilities of the large part of humanity, if we judge by both the physical conditions of the populace where these architectural caryatids are situated and their social conduct. Jean Genet (*The Balcony*) was so perceptive:

What are these structures but private mausoleums, paeans to human vanity at the expense of social actualities? So the question remains Why? What is the justifying rationale, viewed from the perspective of the millions of beggars that litter the streets of those countries, the hit-or-miss level of their health delivery services or indeed the accessibility of the most basic structures of self-fulfillment for their teeming generations in a modern, competitive world? We know that the foreign architectural consortiums benefit. They hone their skills on these engineering challenges and swell their capital reserves by billions of whatever currency in which they elect to be paid. Their skilled workforces are guaranteed a livelihood for years. But the nationals themselves? Apart from unskilled labor, just what do they productively contribute? What level of integrated development does the nation gain? How interactive are such structures in the enhancement of the daily quality of life?

It is against the background of such travesties that one grabs deliriously at the first paragraph of the preamble of a United Nations document, none other than the final presentation by African Ministers Responsible for Human Development toward the March '95 Copenhagen Conference. This paragraph goes to the heart of my contention and relieves me and others in my position of assuming burdens that really belong to others. It is a curious tendency altogether. Obvious truths, especially when they carry the flavor or implication of an accusation, of a dereliction of responsibilities, a misdirection of social endeavors, tend to arouse combative responses in governments when they come from writers or intellectuals. It is a wearisomely familiar self-defensive reflex, one that manifests itself in those demonizing expressions "utopian," "unrealistic," "cloud cuckooland," even that catchall dismissive taunt "obviously Westernized thinking." Those who most frequently award such attributes, usually spokesmen of African governments and a handful of

Establishment intellectuals, the superpatriots, little realize, alas, that they insult history and discredit their own race by the attribution of humanistic principles solely to the Western world. We are accustomed to those knowing, even patronizing winks and nods that supposedly imbue such agents of government policies with the benefit of inside knowledge, a superior foundation of experience, et cetera—all of which guarantee that the implicit accusations or questions are never answered, only deflected, and the propositions evaded as something only to be expected from those "alienated minds." Well, it does appear that a reformation in thinking has been taking place in those very uncontaminated minds in recent times! Is it all convenient rhetoric, an attempt to sanitize the disreputable power images that they represent before those far more potent powers from whom aid or cooperation is solicited? We shall insist on taking their statements at face value.

And so, disowning any claim to originality and employing the very words of bureaucrats, technocrats, and politicians, the following is what must be accounted the coincidence of their views of the human entity within any developmental concept, at long last, with its evolution in other societies through centuries to this present threshold of a new millennium:

We, the Governments of African countries represented by our ministers responsible for human and social development, meeting in Addis Ababa on 20 and 21 January 1994 as a preparatory regional conference on the World Summit for Social Development to be held in Copenhagen, Denmark, during 6 to 12 March 1995, resolutely affirm the centrality of the human being as the initiator and beneficiary of development, the means and the end, the agent through whom and for whom, all development activities must be undertaken.

So, what's new? Nothing, except of course the source from which this declaration has emerged—WE, THE GOVERNMENTS OF

AFRICAN COUNTRIES! We may never hear it again, so let us celebrate the welcome aberration, hoping it has not earned many of
its formulators the sack or worse. This declaration, in my view,
represents a final convergence of nation definition and fundamental expectations between the rulers and the ruled, between
the leaders and the led. For what else, on their part, have the
latter ever claimed? On what other platform have they ever
agitated? For what other cause have they suffered imprisonment,
torture, exile, even death? Examine that summative declaration of faith how you will, under whatever ideological prism
or sententious hairsplitting, and from whatever terrain—from
former apartheid South Africa through former Communist orthodoxies to the present scourge of fundamentalist insanity
that now threatens to coerce the world into its own demonic
closure of nation being—the essence of that declaration has
remained one constant factor, one bedrock against which every
creed, every ideology, every racist philosophy, every inbreeding
personality cult of power has been hurled again and again
in murderous tidal waves. That bedrock has not budged and
its adherents have clung to it like limpets, defying the direc-
tion-changing storms of ideological imperatives. Millions have
drowned in those storms, however, let us never forget that.
Millions of that humanity have been swept away, millions have
perished, never really understanding why, never really understanding to what gods they were sacrificed, other than that the
state or the aspiring state had ordered it, that some program in
the cause of a mere concept of nationhood demanded they be
uprooted from their homes, turned into stateless nonpersons,
degraded from creatures of feeling or sentience to mere digits in
some abstract evocation that had become the end, not the means,
to the elevation of humanity, the enhancement of its productive
potential, or the harmonization of its relationship with power
and authority.

We have been compelled to live decades and centuries of lies, propagated often with state violence, lies that are often compelling, since humanity, to its credit, is never content with the limitations of its own material body and immaterial spirit and therefore seeks goals that extend beyond itself, beyond its immediate seizure of and relationship with the world. It is a human characteristic, and myriad, we acknowledge, are the attainments that owe their genesis to this restlessness of the human mind. Alas, there are those individuals who are especially gifted with the exploitation of this craving for human self-enlargement. They are the con-men of society, practiced liars, solipsistic manipulators. They belong to the same tribe of smooth, practiced salesmen who can offload the proverbial shipload of fur-lined polar boots on a tribe of tropical herdsmen and throw in a consignment of snow tires for good measure. That analogy is, I promise you, not far-fetched but borrowed from actuality. Many notions of nation building and development on our continent have proved as relevant to actualities as polar boots on the feet of a Masai herdsman.

Some of these lies are still with us, especially in the territory of the ineffable, called religion. And spaces that were once teeming human habitations are now depopulated because of these compelling projections that overwhelm the material rootedness of millions and their well-being. Wherever, for instance—to return to the physical zone of existence—wherever the nation ideal becomes a notion beyond the centrality of its human composition, where the nation ideal becomes, for instance, conflated with notions of racial purity or other forms of extreme nationalism, we know only too well what the guaranteed consequences have been. We encounter immediately exclusivist policies that go beyond expelling other human units beyond a specific national space; the new imperative demands that they be totally excluded from the category of humanity, and thus from the physical world altogether. Ideological rigidity, religious extremism, racism, or xenophobia—these are all foundations of forms of transcendentalism that result in dire consequences for any people.

We are familiar with all the rationalizing, mythification processes, all predictable. We know the demagoguery that overcomes the susceptible and makes millions submissive to the hypnotic mechanisms of power. From time to time, however, a portion of that same population of victims recover their senses, begin to function again as members of a human collective that has become conscious of having been robbed of its will, ready to contest the robbery and demand restitution. My understanding of the grudging motions toward the replacement of humanity, rather than abstractions, at the center of development, as is demonstrated in the cited declaration of the representatives of African governments (maybe we should frame and hang it up in all public buildings, hospitals, schools, halls, and other structures), my guarded assessment is that perhaps, just perhaps, the mutual admiration club of African leaders is preparing to join the rational world in repudiating this wasteful cycle of loss and recovery and has chosen to begin at the only commencing and terminal point of development that can be universally agreed upon because it is not a projection of the imagination but a material, irreducible factor—the human entity.

In addressing the issues of nationhood and development, therefore, both in definition and as a living project, the immediate question with which we are confronted is this: How is the collectivity of such a unit best organized? Or to begin with what we know, what we observe, live in, die in, and even—as we often console ourselves—die for, how do such entities presently fare, those present groupings of that lowest common denominator, the human unit? Are they working? Or do they work against the constituent units, the humanity? In short, does the superimposed idea "nation" harmonize or conflict with our given a priori, humanity? If not, what are the causes? What are their histories, and what future do such histories further threaten? Some of these questions answer themselves very quickly and with a chastening finality. Rwanda for one. Or Yugoslavia. Or the Sudan. Others permit the luxury of hesitation, some lingering over uncertainties, the weighing of pros and cons, some space for tinkering and time for the claims of redeeming factors. But clearly, the responses to a few so-called nations are stark, unambiguous, and clamorous, even desperate for remedial action.

It is from that human perspective that any national surely pauses periodically and demands, Is mine the ideal state of the nation idea? A question or stocktaking that surely can only be addressed on the material plane. The ledger book is where to look, not any mystery texts of pious intentions or abstract notions. Humanity is not abstract.

We have spoken here of a competitive GNP. Those who think that this alienated concept of humanity was limited, in Africa, to forced labor and distorted production systems, most notoriously under Belgian colonialism, or, further afield, to the dehumanized production collectives of the Soviet Union, had better take a second look at the economic experiments, first in countries like Tanzania and then, to a far more destructive, indeed criminal degree, the forced human displacement programs of Mengistu's Ethiopia, all in the name of ill-digested notions of Marxist economic centralism. But of course we must not attempt to suggest that such impetus in nation building or transformation is always so idealistically motivated, if one may be permitted to abuse that expression in a context that involves, sometimes, the decimation of the very people that contribute toward the attainment of such nation ideals; we need only recall the fate of millions of kulaks under Stalin or indeed the annual trail of skeletons that became the identifying mark of Mengistu's economic policies. We had better not remain strictly within the categories of the idealist builders, however warped such ideals may have proved. There are others at the comic end of the tragicomic axis, those whose recollection of nationhood is triggered alive only during Independence Day or other calendar occasions and sporting events, soccer most especially.

Perhaps I should have said farcical. Comedy sounds too generous a word to describe what often strikes me as a purely jingoistic invocation of one's nation in those spasmodic recollection habits that exclude the apprehension of the nation as a continuous living organism, as one that shares the same basic human component as other near or distant, but evidently productive claimants to that definition. It is difficult to recall, for instance, that a war was actually fought once for the sake of soccer. The nations involved were, I believe, Honduras and the Dominican Republic. This of course supplies us with the quintessence of farce as a promiscuous begetter of tragedy. When one reflects on this normally comatose nationalist agenda, one that is virtually nonexistent in the mind of the ordinary toiling peasant or worker, but for which he is called upon to kill and be killed at the whim of a dictator (Pinochet comes most readily to mind) the words of the Anglo-Irish poet and playwright William Butler Yeats come readily to mind. Said Yeats: "State and nation are the work of intellect, and when you consider what comes before and after them, they are not worth the blade of grass God gives for the nest of the linnet." Sobering words, for the recollection of which I must thank Denis Healey in a recent article in the *London Sunday Times*. Also for the reminder that Yeats was a fierce nationalist in his early writings who, however, came toward the end of his life to recognize nationalism as "a dangerous illusion." It can of course also be a farcical illusion, an opportunist, purely adventurist evocation, with tragic overtones, which is where we are at the moment, and which compels us to acknowledge the impassable gulf in nation apprehension between African forms of leadership, the dictatorships most notoriously, and the populace itself.

So, moving lower down from divine architecture to mundane, bruising preoccupations—how else would one explain why a ruler over an impoverished, bankrupt state seeks to deplete that nation's resources even further for the sole purpose of staging a World Cup event on its tortured soil? Of course it has to do yet again with the need for national self-assertion, a somnambulist response to a decaying reality, where the undertaker of a moribund nation suddenly wakes up to the existence of an entity he hardly comprehends, only that it shares a category called nationhood with others and is therefore entitled to contest certain functions with them—in this instance, sports.

For fear the point may be missed, let me belabor it without apologies: In the conception of such a ruler, a junior World Cup Finals on his own soil, presided over by his person, is the equivalent of the basilica of Yamoussoukro or the grand mosque of Casablanca. It is a triumphal arch that magnifies his puny being, a perpetual mausoleum within legend that monumentalizes his otherwise unremarkable passage.

The African nation, alas, is mostly viewed through the goggles of such rulership, in studied contrast to the far more organic, comprehensive apprehension of that word when applied to entities like France, Sweden, Japan, Italy, South Korea—alas, mostly the European nations, a few Asian, or the American. It is the confidence, the taken-for-grantedness of such nation entities that makes it possible for them to embark upon new arrangements—even with all the attendant bickering and retreats—such as the European Union, to argue over serious and petty details, to be even "nationalist," but in a concrete sense beyond the slogan of defending "national sovereignty," protecting "our way of life," protecting trade, fishing rights, jobs, labor standards, and contrasting their nation actualities in a positive manner with that of the "frogs," "the blimeys," "krauts," "garlic eaters," and others. What, by contrast, has a geographical space such as Sierra Leone or Gabon or Nigeria come to mean, in concrete terms, when a leader speaks of "national sovereignty"? Is that by any chance an expression that has the slightest impact on the market woman or the factory worker who sees the buying power of the nation's currency dwindle to nothing, health a luxury reserved strictly for the affluent and exhibitionist cronies of power, and social opportunity the hereditary preserves of their pampered scions? Does it go beyond an echo, voided of substance once it has left the mouth of an incumbent dictator? A nation is a collective enterprise; outside of that, it is mostly a gambling space for the opportunism and adventurism of power.

Now let us ask ourselves which of these perspectives express the Nigeria that we know today. What is the social reality as experienced by the inhabitants of that space into which a soccer basilica was about to be intruded? Is it by any chance free of the population of beggars that crowd Casablanca or Yamoussoukro? Of vast sections of disease-ridden humanity? Are the faces we encounter radiant with hope and confidence in their future or masked with fear and uncertainty?

The response is stark and unambiguous, but let us begin by re-collecting that it was not always so, that, fortunately, there are those who recall a social cohabitation that was not riven by the present uncertainties. It is difficult for instance to recall that there were times when religion was a harmonizing factor even between communities of different faiths, that a spiritual richness pervaded daily existence no matter whether it came from the Moslem, traditional, or Christian social and religious structures and observances. The use to which religion is put today (and we speak here not merely of extremists but of government complicity) often translates directly into politics, both local and national. The nature of such politics does not require much effort to envisage.

There have been too many lost moments, moments when this particular disease could have been firmly rooted out, when leadership chose instead to exacerbate such divisions for its own agenda of control rather than set an example in the harmonization of faiths. We are speaking, to name a concrete instance, of a nation of multiple faiths that has yet to recover from the effects of the mad adventure of being dragged into corporate, national membership of the Organization of Islamic Councils under the dictator Ibrahim Babangida. It is not a question of whether or not membership of such a council would be advantageous in some form or the other to sections of the nation or even the nation as a whole (aid and soft loans from Islamic states, commercial privileges, et cetera) but simply that this was one headache, one mightily explosive distraction that the nation could have done without. It was a move that was bound to divide the nation and exacerbate sectarian suspicions, which of course it abundantly did. Religiosity has very little to do with nation-to-nation embrace of whatever kind, and certainly even less to do with those that carry the slightest suspicion of political overtones. The reverberations of such a move, however, what you might call the ripple effects, continue to plague Nigeria today, encouraging a disruptive militancy in some and a disruptive counter-response in the rest. But let us not remain too long in the spiritual realm. The agony of a nation is observable largely in material reality, which alone records its proof of existence. Now, how is that reality actually experienced by the Nigerian people on a daily basis? Let us begin with the forum for the exchange and dissemination of ideas and social awareness, one that at least guarantees a measure of participation in the flow of life within any community.

The press, that once vibrant voice of the Nigerian nation, is officially dead, wiped out in one fell swoop, unprecedented in the history of Nigeria, by the present dictator, Sani Abacha. Apart from the valiant remnant of that press, functioning with an erratic sword grazing its neck, the nation's voice is contracted to two newspapers run by the government (one of them bankrupted by lack of readership) as well as the electronic media, across which that dictatorship has placed a stranglehold. The once stimulating, provocative discourse of a nation of at least ninety million people is reduced to the mendacious bleats of the neolithic occupant of Aso Rock, the seat of government, and the relay system of his sycophantic train. But the existence of a vigorous risk-taking underground press speaks volumes, and this remains one of those signs that inform us that the combative spirit of a nation is not yet extinguished.

The health services of that nation are nonexistent; mothers die in childbirth for lack of the most basic drugs and a hygienic environment for labor. Infant mortality has reached epidemic proportions. The simplest, easily curable disease worsens for lack of treatment and kills. Three years ago, even a military governor, a pillar of the establishment, lamented that the hospitals in that country had become mere consulting clinics, so desperate had become the dearth of basic drugs and hospital equipment. Two years later, that is, last year, a medical specialist, also in the service of government, was compelled to return to that statement, updating it with the comment that the nation's hospitals could no longer claim even that downgraded status but had become virtual mortuaries.

Potable water, even in the heart of the nation's capital, has become a commodity that is left to the dispensation of the skies, from where, perhaps, it is also hoped that Sango, the god of lightning, would perform the miracle that has so far eluded an infamous institution known as NEPA, the Nigerian Electric Power Authority. (Nigerians have even become bored with the game of finding new readings for that acronym, the best known being "Never Electric Power Anytime.") Many small businesses have collapsed as a result of this failure and often join domestic households in mourning the periodic vengeful surges of power that incinerate their appliances and even their homes, as if the god of lightning has indeed taken personal charge but remains unschooled in the elementary laws of voltage distribution. The generator trade—not industry!—booms, however, the market monopolized at the top by the very public servants and their fronts who are paid from the public purse for the supply of electric power.

Public transportation is so inadequate that it provides a study in collective masochism, degenerating often into a contest of the survival of the fittest at the arrival of the lone tumbril. In certain suburban areas—Oshodi, Apapa, Ipaja, for instance—workers on a seven-thirty to five o'clock shift must leave home at four in the morning and are lucky to be home at eight or nine in the evening. The sight of in-between commuters listlessly awaiting some form of locomotion on a blistering Lagos afternoon at improvised stops without shelter, while the latest off-the-line models in private automobiles cruise by, strikes visitors no less forcibly than those who still guard their conscience among the privileged of such a national space. It is over twenty years since I wrote *Opera Wonyosi,* and while the social condition of people had not then truly deteriorated to the present level of despair, this easily managed condition remained so aggravating that I accorded it a verse in the play:

> Have you seen those workers daily jostling
> To catch a bus to beat the factory deadline?
> And the pregnant mother wedged with elbows
> Barely dodging those haphazard blows?
> You'll claim the boss is also on the breadline
> The "go-slow" has wrecked his daily hustling
> Well, a whole day in an air-conditioned car
> Is sweeter than one hour in over-heated air.
>> Explain the smugness on the face of the chauffeur
>> He knows that at the bus-stop, life is even rougher.

Today, a different kind of language would be required to address this violation of the human essence!

And education? Tertiary institutions have fallen below the level of secondary schools. Let us take good note of this by the way; it is a statement that will be re-echoed later within that same declaration of African government spokesmen, while hundreds of thousands of youths roam the streets, jobless, without purpose or direction, half-baked products of secondary and tertiary institutions.

Hunger stalks the streets and, with it, desperation. Thus, security of individuals has become a game of Russian roulette: One never knows whose turn it is. Even diplomats have been compelled to lead protest delegations to the seat of government in Abuja as, be it on the open road, in the heart of the city, or in their residences, they regularly discover the limitations of diplomatic immunity. It is trite consolation that, unlike journalists, writers, and women in Algeria under fundamentalist malevolence, the average Nigerian citizen in the larger cities or compelled to travel the open road has not begun to write his obituary in advance. But some do dictate, with a fatalistic effort at gallows humor, their last will and testament before leaving home. Yet the country that serves us here as a model is poor neither in human nor in material resources. Only last year, a government-appointed commission of inquiry concluded that over twelve billion dollars, the windfall in oil revenue from the recent Gulf War, was missing, unaccounted for. And millions more continue to vanish every day, in magical disappearance or in misdirected ventures.

Now, that is daily actuality of the environment from which a dictator and his yes-men, without a shred of embarrassment, presumed to launch the rags of nation identity onto the international arena. From a comatose habituation, those who claim to articulate the national will are suddenly aroused to the potential privileges of a living organism. Like long-deprived drug addicts

injected with their favorite poison, they are jerked into consciousness and realize "Oh yes, of course, we are a nation, and
we have national rights. And we must assert ourselves as a
nation. And we must put the nation on the world map"—oh, that
mangy, flea-infested flag that the sanctimonious nationalist
drapes around his torso to cover a repulsive nudity!

All those who disagree are subversives and traitors and lackeys
of foreign governments. The world tournament stays here, even
if we bankrupt the nation in the process. It entails further
degradation of the quality of existence for our people since, of
course, we must stick our fists down their throats and pull out
the day's lone morsel that the citizen has succeeded in scroung-
ing from dung heaps, but so be it. Somebody must pay for our
moment of national accreditation. Not so, however, said the
people. There is no nation within this space to host the junior
World Cup championships, no, not in 1995. And they took to the
streets, and three days of fasting were ordered by church and
mosque leaders within the so-called national borders, and the
band of "traitors," "national saboteurs," and "unpatriotic elements" swelled both at home and abroad until the soccer club of
nations began to take note and was compelled to relocate its
fiesta. From Nigeria to tiny Qatar—quite a comedown for the
self-vaunting giant of Africa!

I stated earlier that it was not always so; it is good to remember
this. So how did it all go so badly wrong? I am bound to prolong
this focus on my immediate geopolitical constituency, Nigeria,
recalling that for many of my generation, however, that constituency was not always that restricted but was indeed a continental
state of self-identification. I know that as we came into self-
awareness as productive beings, we brought our immediate national space into perspective, not narrowly as an idea from which
we took a sociopolitical definition of ourselves but as a branch of
an even larger idea, the idea of a continental identity in formation.

Such nationalist vision as we had transcended our own boundaries. Many students of my generation surely set their political
sights on variants of a continental oneness; the colonial settler
régimes of East Africa, not to mention apartheid South Africa in
particular, dictated this racial challenge. We were destined (this
much appeared so gloriously clear to us), our destiny was to be at
the forefront of Africa's version of the International Brigade. Our
liberation hordes would sweep down from Ghana, Nigeria, the
Cameroons to engulf the colonial settler régimes of Kenya, the
Rhodesias, stopping only at the most provocative tip of the
continent—South Africa—whose apartheid philosophy and policies had moved beyond the terrain of experimentation to the most
extreme, hallucinatory edges of dehumanization. (What color are
the hands that dehumanize our African peoples today, as they
have done for nearly four decades of independence?)

In between, the forests of Kenya were already sutured with the
elusive motions of the Mau-Mau liberation forces, crisscrossed
by British colonial hounds in desperate pursuit. Where these
motions intersected in time, the result was death or misery in
British detention camps. Heirs to various pan-African movements, beginning with the famous Manchester gathering of 1945,
Nigerian, Ghanaian, and East African students debated news
from these and other stubborn enclaves, viewing them as assaults
on both racial and national pride. So deep was this sense of total
repossession that our nationalists, in Nigeria at least, sang
the praises of the mosquito, crediting that malaria-dispensing
scourge with the failure of the European colonizer to occupy the
west with the same settler lust as was inflicted on East and South
Africa. Let me sum up this vision of the nationalists, a vision that
was to be fulfilled by the liberation forces of which we were
destined to be the vanguard: We saw the continent, at least from
the south of the Sahara to the southern tip of the continent, not
as a conglomeration of nations but as one nation, one people.

For that same Nigeria, however—and this is certainly true of the Ghanaian, the Senegalese (with its Arab/Mauritanian complication), the Malian, Kenyan, Malawian, and Zairois—the boundaries of a communal identity are today set much more narrowly. The sights of the average nationalist are sadly contracted. The reason is simple: There is so much work to do, and charity, it is said, begins at home. Most Nigerians of the pan-Africanist temper have moved away from the continental shelf to the boundaries of colonial endowment, desperate for a salvage operation of what is closest at hand. In some cases—and here we come to the real predicament—that national capsule is even seen to have cracked internally, and the watchers have begun a drastic interrogation of history, of the beginnings and affective meaning of the nation identity. It is not an elevating development, and it is one that many in well-insulated compartments of governance prefer to pretend does not exist, but it is real! Despite the pains of any official ostrich, it is only too real and, for us in Nigeria, it commenced over the past decade and has dominated public discourse most critically in the past two or three years. The precise, immediate cause of the phenomenon was the annulment of the elections of June 1993.

Let us hasten to absolve the Nigerian populace, the ruled, almost in its entirety, from this regression into narrowed entities. We must identify the cause where it manifestly is, where it is always to be found, and that is a minority that constantly plays up innately innocuous differences, be they of ethnicity or religion, in order to set one section against another and thus assure itself of political control.

It is customary to declare that man is a political animal. It is a definition to which I subscribe, but for purely strategic reasons. We must insist that man is indeed a political animal if only to give dictators sleepless nights, in order to remind them that they hold sway over a restless breed of their own kind, whom they have deprived of their animal rights and who will one day challenge them, true to type, over this territorial imperative, as usage dictates within the animal kingdom. When, as the fable teaches us, the king of the forest loses all measure of self and demands that its daily prey deliver itself up to him in meek obedience to an agreed-upon roster of consumption, it is time to confront him with the fathomless resource of alternative power and drown him in the arrogance of a delusion.

In a more fundamental sense, however, man is first a cultural being. Before politics, there was clearly culture. Only man the producer could have evolved into the political being, which, to pare away all mystification, is the evolutionary stage related to the development of society and the consequent sophistication acquired in the management and protection of resources. This hierarchy of evolution also explains why man resorts to his cultural affiliations when politics appear to have failed him, never the other way round. The ongoing retreats into real and pseudo-ethnic bonds on the Nigerian political scene, as can also be witnessed in other evolving societies both in Europe (the former Communist empire, especially) and on the African continent, can best be understood in this light. With this reminder, we again address the rock on which the Nigerian ship appears all set to founder—the democratic leap of June 12, 1993!

Any internally robust, well-consolidated capsule can withstand a certain level of stress from within or buffeting from without. For an already distressed enclosure, however, such as we have taken pains to depict as accurately as can be universally attested—one whose inmates nonetheless remain conscious of their own potential—a mere test prod of its casing (again, from within or without) can prove to be more than the mere letting out of noxious gases; it may prove the final, fatal prod, resulting in the quiet collapse of the balloon or the implosive rupture of a deceptively hermetic edifice. "In my father's house, there are many mansions there," runs the spiritual. When any one mansion is prodded toward a recollection of decades of wrong, but more crucially, toward a feeling of a conspiracy by elements within yet another mansion, a conspiracy designed to hold all other mansions down to the deviant's minimalist concept of the potentiality of the entire household, insisting on a restriction of that potency to the dwarf vision of their indolence, their effeteness and unproductive temperament, a minority whose vision of society is an expansive, condescending patronage, one whose relationship even to the inmates of its own specific mansion is that of the hereditary overlord in a tradition of serfdom, then, need we be astonished at the moment when every inmate becomes an uncertificated structural inspector, taps on the walls and reports: "Unsound, decertified for human habitation!"?

Go to the markets, go to the mechanic villages, mingle among the "Area Boys" of Lagos and Kano, travel incognito in a long-distance bus from Agege to Benin, Okene, Abuja, Kaduna, Sokoto, Maiduguri, speak to these "unlettered" inmates of unprivileged mansions of "my father's house," and the object of their rancor is inescapable: one mansion—and not even its entirety, just a chamber (the most luxurious, predictably), but the occupants of that chamber have developed a chronic propensity for alliances with kin interests from other privileged habitations of the total household. And the lifestyle and life mission of these indolent, spoilt scions of the household render insecure the foundations of a simple enterprise of cohabitation. Inevitably, these other dwellers resort to this question: Is it not more sensible to pull the rug from under such pampered feet by establishing our own self-subsisting habitation?

And so, if you pose the question to such sections of that nation today, in the form "Do you believe in Nigeria as a nation?" the answer from many sections, going by the tenor of debate from June 23, 1993, till now—be it within the "mansions" described above or transferred to a formalized "representative" forum, where we objectively analyze the recorded proceedings of the diversionary, spendthrift, so-called Constitutional Conference, a collective insult that was imposed on the nation by the dictator General Sani Abacha to ensure an eternity in office—the response we obtain is weighted on the side of "No!" June 23, 1993, was of course the date when the nation was stunned with the annulment of the presidential election of June 12, an election whose results were already halfway broadcast to the whole world and whose conduct was universally adjudged free and fair by any standards. The perpetrator of this "crime against Nigerian humanity" was none other than the former dictator General Ibrahim Babangida, the then majordomo of that feudal mansion that is resolved to impose its anachronistic and undisciplined vision of housekeeping on the rest of the family compound.

At best, to return to our question, we might receive an ambiguous, qualified "Yes," hedged about with conditions, but those who wish to be truthful to the evidence of their hearing must admit that the mood of the nation, in the main, amounts at best to a vote for the reconsideration of the nation status as it now exists. The irony is that it was not the Nigerian populace that repudiated nationhood; on the contrary, they expressed, on that day of June 12, a clear desire for nothing else. It was this numerically infinitesimal but well-positioned minority, blinded by self-interest, seeing that a nation was about to slip from its hands and be restored to a majority dispensation, that commenced the destruction of all sense of belonging. It is that same minuscule proportion who, having succeeded in robbing the Nigerian people of their nationhood (at least for now), insist, with the dismally predictable collaboration of their foreign, traditional (colonial) backers, and in face of daily stubborn evidence to the contrary, that the famed election of June 12, 1993, is ancient history. Alas, if that election of June 12 proves indeed to be ancient history, then—and do take this as prophecy—Nigeria as a nation has no future history.

The undertakers of that date and its actualities, and their apologists, plead a pragmatism that only they appear to understand. The mandate given to Nigeria's president-elect, Bashorun M. K. O. Abiola, they insist, has become tainted with the passage of time. It has become compromised beyond salvage, by events to which, they even claim, that candidate was himself a party. Maybe. Maybe not. The conveniently ignored fundamental issue is that the elections of June 12, 1993, are totally beyond the control or directives of the principals. The apologists of the annulment of that election sadly do not understand where their logic leads. If the will of a nation, freely expressed, attested to by observers from the international community as an exemplary democratic exercise, endorsed even by the monitoring agents appointed by the incumbent régime and by its secret services, if that expression of nation being, since it was a result that cut across all boundaries—ethnic, religious, professional, class, and even across the established parties—if such a ringing declaration of a hunger for nationhood, of a craving for a democratic order, is so tainted as to become invalid, what does that make of the nation whose will is so easily flouted? Any election (to ignore for now the history of this specific one) can prove the cement that binds a nation together or else the porous vessel through which its lifeblood seeps away. If the nation's will has become so tainted that it cannot be implemented, then the nation itself has become so contaminated that it cannot begin to claim the recognition of a nation.

When I find myself cornered by others who pose a similar question to me, "Do you believe in Nigeria as a nation?" my answer is invariably a question "Do you accept my definition of a nation?" And today—praise the deities of the land!—I find my definition endorsed by the declaration of representatives of African governments, lodged in the conclusions now filed with the United Nations. Thus, for the moment, I am able to claim that I accept Nigeria as a duty, that is all. I accept Nigeria as a responsibility, without sentiment. I accept that entity, Nigeria, as a space into which I happen to have been born, and therefore a space within which I am bound to collaborate with fellow occupants in the pursuit of justice and ethical life, to establish a guaranteed access for all to the resources it produces, and to thwart every tendency in any group to act against that determined common denominator of a rational social existence. I accept that space as a space of opportunities and responsibilities that must extend beyond its boundaries, principally because of its rich endowment in material resources. I accept that space as one that is best kept intact, in order to harness those resources with maximum efficiency, conserve and mutually cross-pollinate its cultural hoards, enable it to link hands with others right across to the southern tip of the continent, and present a formidable machinery of collaboration on equal relationship with the rest of the world.

Expressions such as "territorial integrity" and the "sacrosanctity of boundaries," those relics of a colonial master-slave bequest that abjectly glorify the diktat of colonial powers, are meaningless in such a context. The mouthers of geography as an instrument of patriotism belong, in my view, to the class of people referred to by the writer Samuel Johnson, who declared that "patriotism is the last refuge of a scoundrel." What is in it for those within that cordon of geographical patriotism? That, clearly, is the ultimate question and purpose. If one accepts Nigeria as a space that must move beyond what a politician once described as a "mere geographical expression" to what my vision dictates as a humanized space of organic development, then I may be moved to stop quibbling over mere nomenclatures.

Until then, that unfulfilled promise, Nigeria, must remain only a duty. And it is that same duty that we, on our part, must continue to urge upon those same "Governments of African countries," challenging them to realize their own pronouncements, denouncing them before the entire world when they fail to do so, and insisting in that case that they be treated as pariahs, as the real traitors to their own kind and to humanity in general.

Clearly, that space, Nigeria, cannot be the duty and the burden of the writer and the intellectual alone. Indeed, our function is primarily to project those voices that, despite massive repression, continue to place their governments on notice. Additionally, however, we insist that it is time now to move from quiet diplomacy to variants of the same concerted action that brought to its knees one other nation, apartheid South Africa, that refused to accept the universal affirmation that makes the centrality of the human being, without exception of color, class, sex, race or religion, the means and the end, the agent through whom and for whom all development activities must be undertaken.

That declaration, which I persist in attributing to its unlikely source, the representatives of African governments, summarizes the predicament of our society. It recognizes a definite crisis of nation being and furthermore details its contradictory actualities unambiguously through brutal assessments of numerous aspects of national life throughout the continent. The paper identifies, for instance, "a crisis of governance encompassing such well-known shortcomings as the near absence of democratic structures, popular participation, political accountability and transparency." It recognizes that "civil strife is closely associated with challenges to authoritarian structures of government, as well as ethnic and communal confrontations." There, these spokesmen could have added, without contradiction, that such communal confrontations are often deliberately provoked into being by authoritarian régimes in order to create instability, which then justifies repression and an excuse to remain longer in power until "order is restored," "the shattered economy recovers," "a new constitution is written and adopted," "stability is guaranteed," "the crisis," which they fomented, "is resolved," et cetera.

However, our guiding representatives of governments do continue to agree with us, the alienated, nation-denigrating, brainwashed Westerners, negativists, and professional doom-sayers, whose sense of sophistication is simply to pull down their own peoples before Western eyes and so on and so forth. Yes, they join us in observing that "over twenty million Africans are refugees and displaced persons. This represents almost half of the world's refugees." This statistical ignominy appears to be even beyond our own remedy, for within those boundaries, those so-called nations that at least organize their own existence, and upon whose shoulders the responsibility for the relief of their own kind ought to fall, appear indeed unable to salvage their own internal predicaments, so how then can they look beyond their borders to ameliorate the calamity of the flotsam and jetsam of humanity in makeshift refugee camps! No, they must await the next advent of a redeemer in the shape of a Bob Geldof or the United Nations.

The stark reality that cripples rescue efforts from within the continent is acknowledged in the same report:

> Concomitant with the decline in all the indicators of human and social development is the virtual collapse of African institutional capacity. Hospital and health centres lack basic equipment and amenities: schools lack basic teaching aids and necessities such as chalk; African universities and institutions, once the training ground for the region's leaders, professionals and technicians have now become poor performing institutions. The morale of those working in many of these institutions has reached rock bottom. . . .

Now, surely, as I hinted earlier, the litany of "those dissident voices" and that of the government representatives have become really inseparable, one from the other. And thus it goes on and on, the dismal picture of a continent that continues to smile at its image in the mirror while the whole world looks on in tears: "the need to accommodate freedom of opinions, tolerate differences," "the need for full and genuine participation in the political, economic and social processes of their countries," the need for the positive side of a revival of religious practices and beliefs, *in so far as tolerance can be inculcated,* as a crucial dimension of religious culture. That dimension has of course become a matter of life and death for the individual, for groups, for women especially, and consequently a matter of life and death for the nation itself. Let us wind up the list of indictments handed down by these government ministers and bureaucrats with the one that concerns us most today: the ignoble and retrogressive role of the military in the African crisis, their wastrel, unaccounted-for spending, their corruption, their alienated apprehension of society and nationhood, and their brutal repression of civic aspirations.

Here at least we may be able to reassure these official critics, who may feel uncomfortable about the kind of company in which they now find themselves, that they can find far more respectable and still African support in the office of the secretary-general of the Commonwealth of Nations, now held by Chief Emeka Anyaoku. In his address in Abuja, Nigeria, on the occasion of the first memorial lecture in honor of the first elected head of a Nigerian government, the late Sir Abubakar Tafawa Balewa, Chief Anyaoku brandished a score sheet of catastrophic grades for military régimes as one long record of incontinence and inbuilt instability. The function of the military, he emphasized, is to defend the state against external aggression, not dabble in the political life of a people, employing violence to camouflage its ignorance of the complex forces that guarantee and sustain the human organism that we describe as a nation.

The sudden, unprecedented surge in the populations of those earlier-mentioned refugee camps, boosted by the unspeakable dimension of genocide perpetrated in Rwanda, pulls us up short. It would rebuke as self-indulgence even the foregoing illustrations of failed nationhood except that they are intended as a warning, a cry for help in averting a similar catastrophe. Prophecy is not my line of business, but a hard question is being posed by events of unprecedented inhumanity, and not only in that benighted part of the world called Rwanda. As I speak, the routed Hutu army is regrouping, infiltrating, its notorious militia readying itself to complete its interrupted program of "ethnic cleansing." The Rwandan Liberation Front, Tutsi-dominated, has demonstrated that its cadres are not above acts of vengeance. A vicious cycle is the inevitable legacy of generations yet unborn.

In such circumstances, is it really impossible to think the unthinkable? A scourge that terminates half a million souls in a matter of weeks is not an assault that is confined to the directly affected space; it sends ripples of dread through neighboring and even distant spaces with a history of internecine conflicts. Suppress it how you will, the question that is precipitated today in a million thoughtful minds across the continent is "Could it happen here?" And even those who have developed, over centuries or decades, a far more benign way of resolving such conflicts must surely, today, cast a nervous glance over other parts of the world and wonder how soon their resources would be taxed, and how severely, in order to rush aid to those sections of the world where yet another eruption makes urgent claims on their humanity.

To those who have come to take certain social ideals for granted or whose concerns are focused on the more readily intrusive ills of humanity, the clamor of voices for the enthronement of democracy as a condition of social existence throughout the world may sometimes sound a misplaced priority. Hunger is a more readily apprehended reality, so is disease or exposure in any form to the unmediated ravages of nature. The sight of skeleton trails across the landscape of the continent, the swollen bellies of malnourished children, or images of entire villages in East Africa devastated by the scourge of AIDS appear far more pressing and demanding of global attention than some peripheral notion of governance called democracy. Indeed, we are accustomed even to the reduction of much of Africa's problems to one of ethnicity, and certainly, slaughter slabs such as Rwanda lend force to this circumscription of social complexities into easily digestible, even if unpalatable capsules. The result is that we are sometimes assailed by voices that have grown so insolently patronizing as to declare that Africans do not really care who governs them or how, as long as they are guaranteed freedom from diseases, shelter, and three square meals a day. I have answered this reductive proposition of the African political personality in other places. I do not propose to give one more second to such racial slurs, least of all when they are given voice from our own kith and kin in positions of, or slurping from the bloodied trough of, power.

We propose instead that, much as those negative facets of existence are contributory to social retardation in their own right, a common denominator of crisis in many areas may actually be found in the refusal of a section—be this understood in terms of class, ethnic grouping, profession, or religion—to grant others the simple right of participation in the process of deciding a collective destiny. The military dictatorships of the African continent, parasitic, unproductive, totally devoid of social commitment or vision, are an expression of this exclusionist mentality of a handful; so are those immediately postcolonial monopolies that parade themselves as single-party states. To exclude the sentient plurality of any society from the right of decision in the structuring of their own lives is an attempt to anesthetize, turn comatose, indeed idiotize society, which of course is a supreme irony, since the proven idiots of our post-colonial experience have been, indeed still are, largely to be found among the military dictators. I do not suggest that the level of intelligence of the military in general is any lower than that of the civil society; no, we have evidence to the contrary. I merely propose that it is the dregs who, against all natural laws, appear to rise to the top: Just take a look around and backwards (Sergeant Samuel Doe, Idi Amin, Jean-Bedel Bokassa, and their ilk) and the latest contribution to that company from my own native land, General Idi Sani Abacha! That phenomenon is one field I shall leave to military sociologists to tackle; I have my own theories, but they will keep for now.

Under a dictatorship, a nation ceases to exist. All that remains is a fiefdom, a planet of slaves regimented by aliens from outer space. The appropriate cinematic equivalent would be those grade B movies about alien body-snatchers. The only weapon of resistance that is left intact is a cultural memory. Make a careful study of people under a dictatorship, and invariably you will observe that it marks a period of internal retreat into cultural identities.

This process is entirely logical; the essence of nationhood has gone underground and taken refuge in that primary constituency of human association, the cultural bastion. And the longer the dictatorship lasts, the more tenacious becomes the hold of that cultural nationalism, attracting to itself all the allegiance, social relevance, and visceral identification that once belonged to the larger nation. That is the painful lesson that the former Soviet empire has for the world. It is the continuing lesson of the Sudan, if the world would only remove the blinkers from its eyes and unstuff its ears! Our acceptance of the centrality of the human entity in a rational social order assumes implicitly and comprehensively all elements that go into the making of that human entity, and these include intelligence and the capacity for choice. These attributes are violated from the moment of dictatorship, and the populace becomes, by definition, a collection of mutants. To regain their wholeness, they withdraw into the cultural sheath; it remolds their psyche, restores their sense of worth.

A dictatorship does not, as we have seen, merely annul the process of choice and participation, which might take the form of an election; it annuls, effectively, the nation itself. If therefore there is an organization that claims to be a club of nations, what, may we ask, are dictators doing within such an organization? What nations exactly do they represent? A rubber, timber, or mining concession granted to an entrepreneur for exploitation also involves the making and implementing of local laws for the survival and profits of the company. It may involve the construction of independent airfields, establishment of company police, public levies or other forms of taxation, or capital-intensive and autonomous infrastructures. The tin mining enclaves of Jos in the plateau region of northern Nigeria until some years ago, or the contemporary high-tech Brazilian jungle lords, violating virgin spaces and wreaking ecological devastation, are pertinent exemplars, but does any or all of this turn such spaces into nations? What makes the American businessman's private army in the Andean jungle depths any more alien to that environment than a power-crazed drug warlord, an indigene of Nigerian or any other space, who happens to have succeeded in seizing control of a section of a nation's armed forces and cows the rest into submission through torture, threat of dismissals, imprisonments, and secret executions? Is such a being a representative voice of a nation? It is time this question is invoked within the United Nations. All organisms evolve, and so must the UNO.

The revolt against the denial of the innate potential of every human unit of society is certainly one of the most crucial elements in the evolution of scenarios that still plague the African continent in those intractable spots of Liberia, spilling over into neighboring countries and derailing the already-rickety train of economic recovery in that region. Somalia still is, while Ethiopia-Eritrea was, an erstwhile victim of this impulsion, leaving much of the economy of the Horn of Africa in shambles and its population yet to recover from a decades-old trauma. Sudan, that much-neglected space of a singularly brutal and fanatic form of dictatorship and repression, is a continuing rebuke to the conscience of the world, but particularly to that of the African continent. And those who care to analyze dispassionately the surge of the politics of religious fanaticism that menaces the peace of the world will make the uncomfortable discovery that this phenomenon is not so much about religion, faith, or piety, but about power, domination, and its complementary idiotization project unleashed on the rest of thinking humanity. Sudan, let us face this in all honesty, is not one nation, never has been, any more than Ethiopia could ever justly or successfully claim to embrace Eritrea. A democratic Ethiopia has recognized that revolution is not merely heroism on the battlefield but the cultivation of the far more profound heroic cast of mind. Not only has the new government conceded to Eritrea the right to recover and actualize her nationhood, Ethiopia has gone further and entrenched in her constitution the right of any of its human groupings to aspire to their own nationhood, as long as the will of such peoples is faithfully established.

When we espouse the cause of democracy, therefore, our minds encompass more than the ritual of the polling booth and the change of baton at the end of an agreed-upon number of years. Side by side with the eradication of the uniformed mutants who erupt from time to time on our national landscapes, we consider also a dispensation that enables all humanity to breathe freely, to associate freely, to think freely, and to believe or not believe without a threat to their existence and without discrimination in their social rights. Implicit in that freedom of association is, difficult as it may be to accept, the right of collective dissociation. The Canadians, till today, have yet to resolve the question of their own single or dual nationhood, and no exponent of either choice has been advertised as some species of retarded development. The price that is being extracted from the people of Chechnya today for their choice of association should be unacceptable to the historic lessons acquired by the twenty-first-century mind. It is primitive, even prehistoric, to have unleashed such brutality on a section of a contested collectivity. Nothing justifies such a savagery of subjugation, carried out regardless of the innocent and nonpartisan in this dispute. Just as primitive is the thirty-year-long struggle of the Sudanese people to decide the conditions of their social existence and the primacy of their religious beliefs.

Despite the emphasis of most of the preceding on the internal realities that uphold or belie the claims of nationhood and the need for a redefinition of such a social organism, based on the conditions of its inmates and their relationship to power and leadership, I remain inclined to sound the concluding note through a conviction that the time has come for a structured pattern of regional conferences on the national question in numerous sectors of the globe, and most especially those sectors whose propaganda machinery effectively denies the existence of such a question, whose state violence ruthlessly silences the restive inmates of what amounts to vast prison yards. While a number of such conferences may prove fruitless, it is quite possible that a few may actually succeed in heading off the débâcle of Somalia, the horrors of Yugoslavia, or the reversion to a hitherto unthinkable, primitive bestiality of Rwanda. It is time for self-defining nations to swallow their pride and redefine their assumptions, but only from the rigorous view of the well-being of millions who constitute their humanity not from the games of power that constantly seeks to aggrandize, to bloat itself through dubious claims on resources, on the illusions of status conferment from mere spatiality, religious mandate, ethnic purity, or domination over potential killing fields.

The history of many nations is so flawed that it screams out constantly for redress. Let us therefore summarize the lessons of that history in all objectivity, keeping out the jingoism that attends the traditional line of thinking to which we are largely habituated: Neither the tenacity of state repression nor the longevity of an illusion is adequate to guarantee an eternity to nationhood whose foundations are unsound and whose superstructures, however seductive, are constantly stressed as much by the incubus of collective memory as by the dynamics of human development, both the quantifiable aspects and the intangible. I believe that the human mind can encompass this recognition in an original, revitalizing way, enabling us to map, literally, new directions that redress the history of societies and humanize the destiny of their peoples.

And what is such "re-mapping" for a nation to whom belongs, justly, the last word, having directly provoked these reflections? An ethical map offers itself, in the Nigerian case, as the painless alternative to the physical remapping, and the ethical test was concluded on June 12, 1993. The course that was set on that day must be pursued if the geographical map is not to prove a mere disposable parchment that will be ripped apart by events. The strain is already evident and every day brings closer our direst predictions. The hands of the nation clock were stopped on a day that, ironically, recorded its birth. If the nation is to live, its resuscitation must commence where its heart first stopped beating.

Epilogue: Death of an Activist

On May 21, 1994, four traditional chiefs were brutally hacked to death during a public rally of the Movement for the Salvation of the Ogoni People (MOSOP). The president of that movement, Ken Saro-Wiwa, was not present, having indeed been prevented by the police who turned him back at a roadblock on security grounds. Later, that same Ken Saro-Wiwa was arrested and charged with complicity in the murders of the chiefs, together with nine other members of the radical wing of MOSOP.

A special tribunal, handpicked by General Sani Abacha, was convened on January 16, 1995, and eventually began sitting in early March after several false starts. One such delay, lasting several weeks, was caused by the admission of two principal prosecution witnesses that they had been bribed by the authorities to give

false evidence against the accused. The defence lawyers, additionally, were routinely harassed and assaulted by security agents
at roadblocks and around the court premises, access to their
clients being rationed at the whim of government agents. The
principal defense counsel, Gani Fawehinmi, had his chambers
machine-gunned by men in military uniform, his guards sustain-
ing severe injuries that led to amputations and one fatality.

None of this deterred them but, in the end, the bias of the
tribunal was so blatant that the defense team withdrew, declaring that their continued participation would only give a sem-
blance of legality to a patent circus spectacle. Among several
others, including both Nigerian and outsiders, an international
observer of the proceedings, Michael Bimbaum, Queen's Council, sent out several despatches, warning that a travesty of justice
was being enacted in the Nigerian city of Port Harcourt. Here
are a few samples from the Q.C.'s observations:

> It is clear that there have been several breaches both of the Nigerian
> constitution and the International Human Rights instruments, to which
> Nigeria is a party.
>
> Mysteriously, a number of witnesses who in their first statements made
> no claim to have seen a killing later identified one or more defendants as
> having committed a killing.
>
> Moreover, in January 1995, both Nkpa and Danwi swore affidavits
> withdrawing their statements, and claiming that they and a number of other
> prosecution witnesses had been bribed to give false evidence.
>
> I concluded that the government wanted a trial before a tame Tribunal. I
> was gravely disturbed by the Tribunal's apparent bias.
>
> The Tribunals have now ruled on submissions of no case to an-
> swer. . . . Two independent observers present when the ruling was given
> commented that it had the ring of a judgement against MOSOP. Having read
> it, I can only agree. The ruling confirms the fear that the Tribunal is strongly
> biased towards the prosecution and the Federal Military government. In my
> view, any verdict of Guilty that it delivers in either trial will have no validity.

Verdict was pronounced on September 30, 1995. As expected, Abacha's Civil Disturbances Tribunal found the writer Ken Saro-Wiwa and eight other MOSOP officals and activists guilty of the murders of four Ogoni chiefs. The sentence: death by hanging. Human rights organisations, statesmen, religious leaders, other public figures, the international press, and governments reacted as expected. Given my early conviction regarding the nature of a degenerate predator in Nigeria's latest dictator, and thus my fears that these victims were doomed, I could respond to requests for comments only with desperate warnings. To the London *Guardian* I replied:

The verdict was, of course, only too predictable. Abacha had decreed the death sentence for Ken Saro-Wiwa, and nothing else. I have tried to convey an actuality in which the judiciary, at nearly all levels, has been subverted, the institutionalisation of secret tribunals whose composition is at the behest of Sani Abacha and his psychopathic core of cronies. I have endeavoured to portray a cynical, single-track mentality, a frustrated, self-cognising pariah who seeks recognition by placing a nation's citizens in constant peril, then sits back with a self-satisfied smirk to savour pleas for clemency.

Let me alert the world however that, unlike the prior exercise,* there is, this time, a very real danger that Abacha will conclude this lethal charade by daring the moral outrage of all intercessors, no matter how detrimental this proves to his own acceptability. Abacha is constantly instructed that the world has learnt to live with horrors, and that one more will make very little difference, at least, in the long run.

Ken Saro-Wiwa is in grave mortal danger. This is no time for pandering to the unpredictable arrogance of a demented dictator. Ken's life will be

---

*The trial and conviction of alleged coup-plotters, which included a former head of state, General Olusegun Obasanjo. Confronted by the very real threats of revolt from sections of the military if the death sentences were carried out, Sani Abacha "bowed to international pressure" and commuted the sentences.

saved only by such immediate, universal action that cripples the illegal authority of Abacha within and outside the confines of Nigeria.

The blows against Nigeria's cohesion have steadily taken their toll and Saro-Wiwa's execution, if that does happen, may prove more than the nation's capsule can withstand. Let Abacha and his murdering cabal be confronted with this stark consequence, and Ken Saro-Wiwa's life may be spared.

On November 7, with a swiftness unprecedented in the history of criminal trials in Nigeria, the final court of appeal—that is, the Provisional Ruling Council—moved to confirm the sentences and ordered the executions of the condemned men. The timing of the confirmation was of course a deliberate show of contempt for world opinion, since the Auckland summit of Commonwealth nations, of which Nigeria was part, was due to begin a few days after the PRC meeting. Sani Abacha's warped imagination presumably revelled in the prospect of inaugurating that summit with the corpses of nine innocent men. Surely the aid of disciplines beyond international relations must be sought to unravel the motivations for this morbid decision and the collective psyche of the soldiers who deliberated and subscribed to the bizarre proceeding. We have already commented on Sani Abacha's mimic propensity; the precedent of Saddam Hussein, who hanged the free-lance journalist, Barzoft, despite world intervention, would be just the kind of model of murderous determination that would appeal to him. Abacha nurses a desperate craving to match and even exceed what he reads as "iron resolve" among his predecessors on the dictator's seat, and the psychopathic disposition, given full rein on a world stage conveniently provided by the Commonwealth summit, must have proved overwhelmingly attractive for his self-preening.

Whatever the explanations, however, in Port Harcourt prison, where the condemned men were held, the prison authorities discovered that there was no willing hangman within reach, and thus Saro-Wiwa and his companions survived a few days longer on death row. It was a brief reprieve, and an ominous one. An executioner was despatched from the north to Port Harcourt, but the levers of death had lain unused for far too long and repeatedly thwarted the hangman, prolonging the agony of the condemned men in a scene of shabby cruelty, an unspeakably inhuman drama. Ken Saro-Wiwa was first among the nine, and it took *five* attempts to hang him. On November 10, as he was led away from the scaffold the third or fourth time, Ken Saro-Wiwa cried out, "Why are you people doing this to me? What sort of a nation is this?"

I received news of the hangings in Tokyo, the morning after I had departed Auckland. Three days later, I still could not bring myself to respond publicly to this crime. The last-ditch efforts to save his life and those of his companions, all the canvassing and hectoring at the Auckland summit, had failed, and there seemed little point in any further commentary. Thanks, eventually, to the appallingly effete response of the Commonwealth heads of states, however, which offered the Nigerian butcher a two-year "ultimatum" to quit office (as opposed to the three which he had already awarded himself in his October declaration), the German journal *Der Spiegel* finally succeeded in breaking through my paralysis and I was finally enabled to visit the charnel house and attempt a reprise of events that led, inexorably, to such a gory conclusion. It was an ironic state in which to find myself, given the days spent impressing on others the very real probability— even certainty—that Abacha would carry out the sentences. Thus, in a way, I had prepared myself for the worst. Perhaps the anguish was really an aspect of Ken Saro-Wiwa's final questioning: *What sort of a nation is this? What sort of a nation is it that permits this? What sort of a nation is this, within which I take my definition?* The focus however, must remain on the factual, external present, and the prospective consequences for a hideous crime against humanity.

There is one immediate question that we need address to ourselves: Why the rush to execution? That question holds the key to the darkest moment in the history of our existence in the benighted nation called Nigeria.

There are hundreds of convicts on the death rows of our prisons, some of them held over ten years, maybe twenty, awaiting their date with destiny. Some are violent armed robbers, cold-blooded murderers. Several are functional sadists, mindless butchers who took advantage of religious or ethnic riots to practise their stock-in-trade. Years after they slaughtered their victims and turned the streets, markets, and especially places of worship into slaughter slabs, years after they were sentenced, they are still kept alive in our prison cells, awaiting rescue by executive clemency. What, then, was the overwhelming cause that drove Sani Abacha—who had taken over the functions of criminal justice, set up his own trial court, then presided over the last court of appeal—to rush Ken Saro-Wiwa and his companions to the gallows? Since when has the cause of justice been served by haste, especially selective justice in its irreversible mode?

In seeking an answer to that question, we would be wise to take our minds back to the internecine strifes, the escalation of mutual destruction, that became a puzzling feature of life among the Delta people over the two years of Abacha's seizure of power in Nigeria. We must remind ourselves of the impersonation of the Okrika, the Andoni, and the Ogoni—all indigenes of the oil-rich Delta region—by Abacha's armed soldiers, the destruction of villages and farmlands, the kidnappings and murders timed to appear as consequences of boundary disputes, mostly minor, but now turned into vicious rounds of bloodletting and serial vengeance among traditionally peaceful neighbours. We must refresh our memories with the detailed reports of commissions of enquiries about this strange and costly eruption of animosity—Professor Claude Ake's meticulous report, as chairman of one such commission, most especially. We must single out, as a chilling and graphic instance, the 1994 machine-gunning of a boat in midstream, in a carefully executed military action that resulted in the deaths of tens of innocent men, women, and children, including prominent citizens of Ogoniland. The Okrika were first blamed for this atrocity, but we recall how the true criminals, proven military personnel, were exposed in the end by the few survivors.

The purpose of Abacha's bloody provocations was straightforward: to make it impossible for the victims of oil exploration to present a united front in their demands for reparations for their polluted land, a fair share in the resources of their land, and a voice in the control of their own development. The Ogoni were, of course, at the head of these agitations.

Still, the Ogoni preserved their united resolve—until lately. The crack in their unity was fomented by the same forces that destroyed the peaceful coexistence of the various communities of the Delta, setting one against the other. The next stage was to set the final seal of doom on the Ogoni, who had had the temerity to spearhead the Delta revolt against the oil companies. Four prominent sons of Ogoni were brutally hacked to death, creating a permanent breach within the Ogoni movement, MOSOP.

Now, there had begun serious moves to heal that breach, with limited glimmerings of hope. I know this firsthand, because I was contacted by both the relations of the murder victims and the peacebrokers. Such a process could only have been initiated as a result of the mounting suspicion that the bloodguilt lay outside the Ogoni community; that, at the very least, the murder of the four Ogoni leaders had been organized by a common enemy, the permanent agents provocateurs in the pay of Abacha's regime. There was only one way to thwart the process of healing within MOSOP, and that was to terminate all efforts to root out the real criminals by speedily offering up more sacrificial lambs from within the same community. This would assuage the thirst for vengeance in the bereaved faction but also widen the blood breach in an irreversible manner.

Ken Saro-Wiwa's fate had long been sealed. The decision to execute him and his eight companions was reached before the special tribunal was ordered to reconvene and pronounce a verdict that had been decided outside that charade of judicial proceeding. The meeting of the Provisional Ruling Council to consider that verdict was a macabre pretence, a prolongation of the cynicism that marked the trial proceedings from the outset.

As the world now knows, the executions were to have taken place immediately after the "ratification" session of the Military Council. Hence the sense of urgency, even panic, with which we addressed our task in Auckland, at the summit of the heads of Commonwealth nations, from the moment that we learnt that Abacha had summoned his uniformed puppets to perform at his dance of death. A blatant, unrepentant defiance of civilised norms, an atavistic psyche is what has characterised this régime from the beginning, so there should have been no cause for surprise. We have warned and pleaded. Now we are paying yet another heavy price for the comatose nature of global conscience.

Is that conscience finally nudged awake? Despite the belated flurry of motions, it appears that the real problem and the solution are still being dodged. Why do the Commonwealth heads of states still proceed to offer Sani Abacha two whole years to "restore" Nigeria to democracy? Nigeria has a civilian president-elect, Bashorun M. K. O. Abiola, clamped in jail by Sani Abacha. We have called for a solution that requires his immediate release in order to head a government of national unity and restore the nation to a democratic path. Every atrocity that has befallen Nigerians, the total collapse of civic society, stems from the pattern of evasion that seeks to find a path around that immutable reality: that Nigerians went to the polls and elected their president, after which a military cabal, of which Sani Abacha was Number Two, nullified that process.*

It is time to stop beating about the bush when a path that, as it happens, combines both principle and pragmatism, opens up itself unambiguously. Yes, of course, there are thorns along that path, a few boulders here and there, but by what yardstick of tolerance or naive optimism can an alternative be proposed in the form of two more years of Abacha? Does any serious-thinking individual believe that the Nigerian nation will survive a two-year endorsement of this national hemorrhage? Let the Commonwealth leaders, the international community, and, most crucially, the nation's own internal collaborators, think again and save the nation from the spiral of murder, torture, and leadership dementia that is surely leading to the disintegration of a once-proud nation.

What sort of a nation is this? We grasp only too painfully what the nation can be, what it deserves to be. If Ken Saro-Wiwa's death-cry does prove, in the end, to have sounded the death-knell of that nation, it would be an act of divine justice richly deserved.

---

*Chinua Achebe, the Nigerian novelist and essayist, expressed this even more succinctly. Ken Saro-Wiwa, he declared, was not killed on the date announced by Sani Abacha's regime, but on June 23, 1993, the day the nation's democratic elections were annulled.

by **Ibrahim Dasuki**
Sultan of Sokoto

~~~~~~~~~~~~~~~~~~~~~~~~~~~~~~~~~~~~~~~

Swear in Abiola

*B*eing *excerpts of a press statement on the state of the nation, by His Eminence, Alhaji Ibrahim Dasuki, CON, LLD Sultan of Sokoto, President General, Supreme Council for Islamic Affairs. Signed on his behalf by His Personal Assistant on Religious Affairs, Alhaji Maman Kolo Zugurma.*

His eminence Alhaji Ibrahim Dasuki is aware of some scathing remarks against the leadership of the Supreme Council for Islamic Affairs over its alleged reticence on the State of the Nation. His eminence has instructed me to state as follows:

1. It is uncharitable for the branches who have made their views known through the pages of newspapers not to have

afforded themselves the usual line of communication which is better than washing our dirty linen in the public. The Council would not allow itself to be stampeded into taken (sic) sentimental decisions.

2. The present political situation is very unfortunate and delicate that provocative emission of words farther than quench the present inferno ranging across the nation may cause more havoc.

3. The Supreme Council for Islamic Affairs not being a political organisation and its tentacles covering all Muslims irrespective of their political leaning must be careful in dabbling into the issue at stake without adequate consultation among our leaders across the country.

4. At the time the council was being criticised for its inertia and clay footedness it was already not only in contact with our leaders across the country but even our respected president, General Ibrahim Babangida. His eminence has directed me further to state that:

a. The Supreme Council for Islamic Affairs believe in the Sovereignty of Nigeria as an entity and therefore would not be party to anything that would endanger the unity of the country.

b. The Council calls on President Babangida whom we believe is a good muslim would not betray the trust of the people of the country and be true to his word to handover power to the civilian on August 27, 1993. He should remember Allah's immutable admonition in the Holy Qu'ran Chapter 4 verse 105:

We have sent down to you the Book in truth that you may judge between men as guided by Allah. So be not used as an advocate by those who betray their trust. But seek for forgiveness from Allah. For Allah is most forgiven Most Merciful.

c. In Islam there is no room for ethnic rivalry for Allah says in the Holy Qu'ran Chapter 49 verse 10 that "All Muslims are brothers" and since the whole world has given a verdict that the election was free and fair and it was the most peaceful in the history of this country there is no other route away from National catastrophe than the swearing in of Alhaji Moshood Abiola come August 27, 1993.

d. Though Alhaji Abiola is seen to be very tolerant to other religious groups in the country he has both financially and morally assisted the propagation of Islam probably more than any other Nigerian in contemporary history and being a National Vice President of the Supreme Council for Islamic Affairs, the Council cannot stand aloof while the whole world is clamouring for him to be declared the winner of the election he actually won.

e. We feel seriously unhappy on the charge that the whole problem is created because a clique in the army is opposed to Abiola being the president of Nigeria. They should remember that Allah says in the Holy Qu'ran Chapter 4 verse 135:

O you who believe stand out firmly for justice as witness to God, even as against yourselves or your parents or your kin and whether it be against rich or poor. For Allah can protect both. Follow not the lust of your hearts lest you swerve, and if you distort justice verily Allah is well acquainted with all that you do.

f. We are very optimistic that our listening president after meetings and consultations with all interest groups in the country will reverse his decision and Alhaji Moshood Abiola Insha Allah be announced as President elect.

g. We call on all Nigerians to remain calm, mind their utterances and cooperate with the Government in coming to an amicable and acceptable solution to the current political impasse.

h. We also appeal to Alhaji Moshood Abiola to regard the present cloudy situation as a test from Allah and he should have absolute faith in Allah and not allow anybody to stampede him into taken (sic) decisions that would lead Nigeria into chaos.

[signed]
ALHAJI MAMAN KOLO ZUGURMA

Abacha's Ultimate Insult:
An Eternal Transition Program *

1995 LAST QUARTER—OCTOBER–DECEMBER

1. Approval of Draft Constitution.
2. Lifting all restrictions on Political Activities.
3. Establishment of the National Electoral Commission of Nigeria (NECON).
4. Creation of:

   Transitional Implementation Committee;
   National Reconciliation Committee;
   Federal Character Commission.

---

*Two years in gestation, delivered in October 1995, swaddled in "shoulds" and "ifs" and a host of conditionalities.

5. Appointment of Panel for Creation of States; Local Governments; Boundary Adjustment.

1996   FIRST QUARTER—JANUARY—MARCH

Election and Inauguration of Local Government Councils on Non-Party basis.

1996   SECOND QUARTER—APRIL—JUNE

1. Creation of States and Local Governments.
2. Commence process of Political Party Registration.

1996   THIRD QUARTER—JULY—SEPTEMBER

1. Registration of Political Parties.
2. Delineation of Constituencies.
3. Production of authentic Voters' Register.

1996   FOURTH QUARTER—OCTOBER—DECEMBER

Election of Local Government Councils at Party level.

1997   FIRST QUARTER—JANUARY—MARCH

1. Inauguration of Party-elected Local Government Councils.
2. Consolidation of new Political Party structures.
3. Tribunal sitting and conduct of any Local Government Bye-Elections.

1997   SECOND QUARTER—APRIL—JUNE

1. Party-State Primaries to select Candidates for State Assembly and Governorship Elections.
2. Screening and Approval of Candidates by the National Electoral Commission of Nigeria.

1997 THIRD QUARTER—JULY–SEPTEMBER

State Assembly Elections.

1997 FOURTH QUARTER—OCTOBER–DECEMBER

1. Election of State Governors.
2. Sitting of State Election Tribunals and Conduct of Bye-Elections.

1998 FIRST QUARTER—JANUARY–MARCH

1. Inauguration of State Assembly and State Governors.
2. Party Primaries to select Candidates for National Assembly Elections.
3. National Assembly Election Campaigns.

1998 SECOND QUARTER—APRIL–JUNE

1. National Assembly Elections.
2. Primaries to select Candidates for Presidential Elections.
3. Commencement of Nationwide Campaigns for the Presidential Elections.

1998 THIRD QUARTER—JULY–SEPTEMBER

Presidential Elections.

1ST OCTOBER 1998

Swearing in of new elected President and Final Disengagement.

Index